# Soviet Sport

# SOVIET SPORT
# BACKGROUND TO THE
# OLYMPICS

## JAMES RIORDAN

Washington Mews Books
A Division of New York University Press
New York *and* London

© James Riordan 1980


First published in the USA by
New York University Press

**Library of Congress Cataloging in Publication Data**

Riordan, James, 1936–
    Soviet sport background to the Olympics.

    1. Sports—Russia.   2. Sports—Social aspects—
Russia.   I. Title.
GV623.R55        796'.0947        79–9689   ⋁
ISBN 0-8147-7382-6
ISBN 0-8147-7383-4 pbk.

Printed in Great Britain

For my brother Terry

# Contents

# Illustrations

# *Acknowledgements*

For permission to reproduce the photographs in this book, Basil Blackwell Publisher is grateful to the following:

Colorsport (page 5)

Novosti Press Agency (title page; pages 8, 12, 37, 69, 94, 104, 133, 149, 157 and 161)

Society for Cultural Relations with the USSR (pages 5, 11, 31, 34 and 118)

Union of Friendship Societies, Moscow (pages 18, 60 and 152)

# Introduction

The 1980 Olympic Games has focused attention on Soviet sport as never before. The occasion is unique, for a communist nation is staging the Olympics for the first time in the eighty-four year history of the modern Games. What is more, the host is the most successful Olympic participant ever. Not only has the USSR 'won' every Olympics, summer and winter, for which it has entered – with the sole exception of 1968 – it is also the most versatile nation in Olympic history, having gained medals in nineteen of the twenty-one sports in the 1976 Montreal Games. A sports system that can consistently achieve such success certainly merits consideration, not least for what it can teach others.

The influence of Soviet sport on the rest of the world is more far-reaching than most countries care to admit. During the inter-war years the Chinese borrowed heavily from Soviet experience; immediately after World War II the Soviet sports structure was largely adopted in all the states of Eastern Europe; in the last two decades extensive assistance in sport has been given to other socialist countries and to many developing states in Africa, Asia and Latin America. Soviet impact on the West is also substantial, as is evident from the largely successful Soviet-backed campaign against apartheid in world sport, the adaptation of Soviet experience in many countries, the re-examination of Western sports policies, increasing exchanges and studies, the fresh perspectives offered by the USSR to international sports bodies, and the choosing of Moscow as the venue for the 1980 Olympics.

In drawing the reader's attention to the generally constructive influence of Soviet sport on the world of sport in general, it is not my purpose to proclaim, 'Look how grand things are there and how dismal in the West!' There are sincere admirers of Soviet sport who question the prominence given in the USSR to the winning of victories, the setting of records and the collecting of trophies; the compromise that has apparently been reached with Western professionalism (the case, for example, of the Soviet tennis players who appear on the American pro circuits) and advertising agencies; the lengths to which some Soviet officials seem prepared to go to achieve success; the double standards that occasionally apply in the definition of professional and amateur status; the 'star' treatment of some performers. Many long-established Western countries still have something to teach the younger nations, including the Soviet Union, about school games, expertise in a number of sports, the provision of public soccer, swimming and tennis amenities and self-organization. The Western nations also have a great deal to learn about the nurturing of talent, sports medicine, industrial hygiene, trade union involvement in sport, the training of coaches, technical and scientific research and much besides, including that essential quality: a willingness to learn.

It has been difficult for those bodies which run sport in the West to grasp what has happened in Soviet sport since the Russian Revolution of 1917. The various changes that have taken place in the socialist states have often confounded those who hold to 'amateur', 'gentlemanly' principles. When a nation decides that the pursuit of sport, free of charge, is the right of everyone, not a privilege to pay for; that as far as status and the development of talent is concerned, sport is on a par with music and art; that the culture of the body is as vital as that of the mind for the harmonious development of the individual and, ultimately, for the health of society – then it is clear we are talking a different language from that commonly spoken by Western sport officials.

It has to be remembered that as Western urban and industrial society grew up, a wide range of sports was invented – or adapted from the pastimes of the nobility – by the so-called middle classes, imbued with their values and designed initially for their training and diversion. With rising living standards and the beginnings of leisure for wider sections of the community, many sports were extended to the working people, some being taken over completely by them (except in their running). In the course of these changes, a number of sports (such as motor racing, tennis, golf, horse racing, soccer and even cricket) became commercialized and adapted for mass consumption, dominated by the profit motive and the needs of a 'sports industry'.

Our own unique pattern of sport, then, is a mirror of our society; it is neither 'natural' nor necessarily 'right' for other people. It is not for general export. Indeed, in societies of scarcity, societies striving to build a new life for mainly illiterate, impoverished peasant populations, Western commercialized sports on the one hand and the gentle-manly dictum 'sport for sport's sake' on the other are often looked upon as entirely unsuitable. Sport in modernizing societies like the Soviet Union is a serious business, with serious functions to perform: it is associated with health, hygiene, defence, patriotism, integration, productivity, international recognition, even nation-building. The Soviet experience of sports development may have more rele-vance to cultural revolutions in the emergent nations of Africa, Asia and Latin America than does our own.

It will be readily apparent that in Soviet sport we are dealing with a philosophy – notably of physical culture – that differs fundamentally from that which we normally associate with competitive sport, or recreation, or physical

education. Physical culture is the parent whose children are
games, outdoor recreation, physical education and competitive sport – even health, hygiene, civil defence and
artistic expression. The acquisition of their culture is an
integral process that accompanies a person throughout life,
in home, nursery, school, college, factory, office and farm.
Consequently, sport in the USSR is by no means a matter
merely of fun and games, something you can take or leave
as you please. Someone who neglects the physical side of
his development is seen as only half a person, like one who
neglects the education of his mind. To Westerners accus-
tomed to the notion that sport is the garden of human
activities, and often a *private* garden at that, Soviet sport is a
revelation. Its study discloses a fresh perspective on the
place of sport in the lives of all members of the community,
one that clarifies why sport in the young Soviet state could
not be allowed to develop haphazardly, as in the West, or
left to the whim of private clubs, businessmen, circus
promoters and rich foreigners, as it was in Russia prior to
1917. Sport is regarded as too important for that. In fact, as
we shall see, sport has been accorded a quite revolutionary
role in the USSR – that of a vehicle of social change.

This book is not confined solely to a description of Soviet
sport; it tries to show too how we in the West can learn from
the Soviet experience and enrich our sport. After all, without a better understanding of sport in other cultures, we
cannot adequately improve ourselves or teach others. In
the first chapter I consider several of the major factors that
have shaped Soviet sport and then, in their light, I suggest
a reconsideration of a number of 'explanations' of Soviet
sport common in the Western media. In the following two
chapters I trace the evolution of the Soviet sports movement from 1917 and examine its present structure. In Chapter 4 I discuss the much-debated issue of talent and then
turn, in Chapter 5, to describe the training of physical
educationalists, coaches and officials. The next two chap-

*School Physical Education class. Development of the body is as vital as education of the mind*

ters give a more detailed picture of two particular sports, gymnastics and soccer. Chapter 7 deals briefly with the topical and complex issue of women in sport, and finally Soviet sport is reviewed in the light of the Olympic movement.

I would like to acknowledge my debt and gratitude to my friends and 'consciences', Don Anthony and Brian Bicat, who read through my manuscript and made valuable comments on my linguistic, sporting and political deficiencies. Finally, with the greatest affection, I dedicate the book to my brother Terry who, for a score of years and more, has shared and sustained my love of soccer and darts and tennis and golf, and has been my companion on the terraces of most English football grounds in support of Portsmouth Football Club. There must be millions of sports lovers like us. And they will understand.

Chapter 1

# Dispelling the Myths

The Russian Revolution of October 1917 marked a break with the past in many ways, but it would be wrong to imagine that after 1917 a totally new structure was created, inspired wholly by new ideas. Soviet sport did not spring fully fledged from the head of Lenin or Marx. The roots of Soviet sport lie deep in Russian history, in the people's habits and traditions, in the climate, in fears about internal and external foes. However, it is also rooted in the organized sports pioneered for urban society largely by Britain, in the gymnastics schools of Germany, Scandinavia and the Czech lands and in Prussian military training. The pattern of Soviet sport has been determined as much by these as by the ideals of a political order.

Before examining its structure in detail, therefore, it will be helpful to look at some aspects of the background to Soviet sport, in so far as they impinge upon its form and development.

*The Physical, Political and Social Background to Soviet Sport*

## GEOGRAPHY AND CLIMATE

The Soviet Union straddles two continents, Europe and Asia. It stretches from the Gulf of Finland in the west to the

Notes are to be found at ends of chapters.

Pacific Ocean in the east (almost within sight of Alaska and Japan). It includes most of the frozen Arctic, yet extends south into deserts bordering on China and Afghanistan. In size it is by far the largest country in the world, covering a sixth of the total land surface of the globe.

The contrasts in its climate, from six months of snow and ice over most of the inhabited part of the country to sub-tropical sunshine in the south, have important implications for the location, season and type of the sports played. In the centre of European Russia, in Moscow, the winter snows normally last from late October to March, with temperatures averaging 10°C below zero in January. January on the Black Sea coast, however, averages 6°C above zero, whereas January in north-east Siberia averages minus 40°C and snow lasts for 200 days in the year.

The long winters over most of the country naturally make skating and skiing the most accessible recreations and proficiency in these sports is of practical value in rural areas.

*Ice fishing. In a land covered in snow and ice for half the year winter sports play a major role*

The long, dark evenings predispose townspeople to indoor games like basketball and volleyball. Throughout the land soccer is played in summer, ice hockey in winter. What is more, the great distances involved in travel influence the location of resources and the regional variations in leagues and competitions.

STRATEGY

The USSR stands not only geographically but also socially and historically between Europe and Asia. Significantly, it shares its frontiers equally with East and West: of its twelve neighbours, six are in Europe (Norway, Finland, Poland, Czechoslovakia, Hungary and Romania) and six are in Asia (Turkey, Iran, Afghanistan, Mongolia, China and North Korea). Such an extensive frontier inevitably creates problems of defence, as the country's battle-scarred history attests.*

The country's geopolitical situation has had two major implications for sport. First, the authorities have used sport quite deliberately to promote friendship with neighbouring states and to cement goodneighbourly relations. Second, given its many borders and its history of invasions, a large standing army is seen as a guarantee of security. Throughout Russian and Soviet history there has been a close relationship between sport and the military, which has helped to ensure that as many citizens as possible are physically fit, mentally alert, trained in military skills (shooting, skiing, etc.) and equipped with the patriotism, will power, stamina and ingenuity that are thought to be essential to military preparedness.

HISTORY

The Soviet Union is European by civil tradition as well as by virtue of its geographical position: European history could

---

* For a map of the area, see p. 85.

not have been written without Russia and the USSR, as Napoleon, Hindenberg and Hitler all discovered to their cost. It is an Asiatic land, however; beyond its window on the West lies an overwhelming hinterland stretching east-wards a quarter of the way around the world, containing peoples who are the sons and daughters of Asia. Today, as at the dawn of history, the country stands at a frontier, embracing half the continent of Europe and over a third of Asia and acting as a bridge between the two.

Most European states share the common cultural herit-age of the ancient Roman Empire and the Catholic Church. Not so Russia. In the tenth century Russia took its religion, alphabet and much besides from Greece – or, to be more exact, from Byzantium. But Byzantium decayed and the centre of advanced civilization shifted to the northern Mediterranean region, leaving Russia outside the main-stream of European development. The Renaissance and Reformation passed it by. In the centuries when Italy had its Dante, Spain its Cervantes, England its Shakespeare and France its Corneille and Racine, the Russian voice was silent. After the fall of Rome and Byzantium the interna-tional cross-fertilization of culture and ideas was mediated by a trade and commerce whose technological basis was maritime. This was generally to the disadvantage of the nations and peoples of Central and Eastern Europe – par-ticularly Russia, with its vast landlocked interior. Thus it is possible to speak of a millennium of economic, cultural and political development in Europe throughout which Russia remained 'a mystery wrapped up in an enigma' – a dark, unknown and unknowing mass.

It was not until the latter part of the nineteenth century that Russia found its voice and astounded the world with the richness and vitality of its literature and music. The West recognized and applauded the genius of such writers as Tolstoy and Chekhov, Turgenev and Dostoevsky, and such composers as Tchaikovsky and Glinka, Borodin and

Rimsky-Korsakov. In sport, too, Russia was beginning to catch up with the Western world by the turn of the century, and the country was one of the founder members of the International Olympic Committee.

## ETHNIC CONSIDERATIONS

The USSR is *not* Russia. It is a multi-national federation of some 270 million people and over a hundred nationalities with widely different traditions, cultures, languages, colour, dress, even religions. For administrative purposes the country is divided into fifteen Union Republics, constituted on the basis of principal nationalities. Many of these national groups are very large; there are, for example, some 140 million Russians, over forty million Ukranians, ten

*Polo in Georgia (Caucasus), one of the many folk-game traditions maintained in this multiethnic country*

million Uzbeks, sizeable groups of Georgians, Tartars, Armenians and Latvians – even Gipsies, Germans and Eskimos. It is therefore both wrong and disrespectful to describe as 'Russian' such athletes as Ludmilla Turishcheva and her husband Valery Borzov (Ukrainians), Olga Korbut (Belorussian), Nelli Kim and Elvira Saadi (Tartars), Levan Tediashvili and Alex Metreveli (Georgians), Jan Talts (Estonian).

*Reindeer racing in Yakutia, a popular year-round sport of Siberia*

Discontent among the national minorities was one of the major causes of the Revolution. Although the Soviet order has brought a great deal of stability and harmony to relations between the various nationalities, nationalism remains a potentially disruptive element in Soviet life.

The implications for sport are, once again, worthy of consideration. National diversity has brought a rich variety of styles and folk traditions to the Soviet sports movement – as in the folk-dance grace of Slav gymnasts, the weightlifting power of the Cossacks and Baltic peoples and the combative skills of Transcaucasian and Siberian wrestlers. World and Olympic wrestling champions Roman Dmitriev and Pavel Pinigin, for example, learned their skills initially in their native Yakut folk *hapsagai* ('sash-wrestling') style, and Olympic champion Levan Tediashvili learned wrestling in Georgian villages where the centuries-old folk wrestling style *chidaoba* is still popular. What is more, inhabitants of the Baltic states of Latvia, Lithuania and Estonia, which were only incorporated into the USSR in 1940, are able to call on the legacy of the YMCA movement of pre-war years; it is, significantly, from this Baltic region that many of the country's top volleyballers still come.

But there is another aspect of nationalism and sport that is of vital concern politically to any developing multi-national state. To the extent that sport can, uniquely, transcend boundaries, it has been employed in the USSR quite explicitly as a means of integration. The Soviet leadership has used it to develop among the diverse peoples not the Russian patriotism encouraged by the tsars but a new Soviet patriotism.

POLITICAL CONSIDERATIONS

The USSR is a modernizing country. We are not dealing here with communist practice in general, but with its application in what was until recently a very backward, semi-feudal country where the most elementary tasks of emancipation had still to be performed, a country in need of industrialization and agricultural modernization to a degree never previously experienced anywhere, a country confronted by the need for the greatest imaginable efforts and sacrifices to be offered in its defence. It is well to remember that it is less than fifty years since some 80 per cent of the population were illiterate peasants whose grandparents had been released from serfdom only sixty years before; since conditions prevailed in which few people survived to 35 years of age and the production of the boundless territory of Russia was less than that of tiny Norway or Switzerland.

In a relatively short time the people have lived through such shattering events as three revolutions, a civil war, foreign intervention, rapid industrialization, forced collectivization of agriculture, purges, mass terror and two world wars. Today most of the population lives in the towns; not only can everyone read and write but far more people per head of population possess a higher education than in any West European country; average life expectancy is 70, on a par with the world's healthiest nations; and the USSR is the second most powerful industrial nation and joint leading military power in the world. And in sport it is without question the world's leading all-round nation.

It has come a long way, perhaps several centuries, in the space of a lifetime.

Once again, the implications for sport of these processes are far-reaching, for sport has been accorded a vital role: it has been designated an agent of social change in the brief period available. Soon after the Revolution sport was taken over by the state and used explicitly for utilitarian purposes: to improve health and raise morale, to develop a fit and disciplined workforce and to provide diversion and recreation for a society that was experiencing a period of rapid change and sacrifice.

International politics also have to be considered. Before the last war, as it was the only communist state in the world, the USSR became isolated from the West and had few contacts with Western governments. The isolation extended to sport. However, the USSR emerged from the war a victor, its power having penetrated Central and Eastern Europe, thus radically altering the balance of power in Europe and the world. Within the space of four years, ten states became aligned with the Soviet Union: Yugoslavia (1945), Bulgaria, Albania, Romania and Hungary (1946),

Poland (1947), Czechoslovakia and North Korea (1948), China and the German Democratic Republic (1949). These were later joined by Cuba, Vietnam, Laos and Cambodia.

In the conditions of international friction or Cold War that developed after World War II, as the two rival military blocs confronted one another in a divided world, sport became an eminently suitable vehicle for international competition, a 'weapon' with which each side could attempt to 'defeat' its ideological opponent. To the Soviet leaders sporting victories over the 'bourgeois' states demonstrated the advantages of the Soviet socialist way of life. As a Soviet source put it six years after the war: 'Every new sports victory is a victory for the Soviet form of society and the socialist sports system; it provides irrefutable proof of the superiority of socialist culture over the decaying culture of the capitalist states.'[1]

In the immediate post-war years Soviet sports associations became affiliated with virtually all the major international federations, and in 1951 the USSR joined the International Olympic Committee. Where other channels have been closed sport has been employed to help attain prestige both at home and abroad. This is a point that is of particular relevance to the emergent nations; it has also been an important stimulus to the sporting commitment of both Cuba and the German Democratic Republic.

## The Role of Soviet Sport: Facts and Fallacies

As we have seen above, the place of sport in Soviet society cannot be properly understood in isolation from consideration of the country's environment and development. Many commentaries on Soviet sport, however, display little understanding of this fundamental fact. What is more, they fail to comprehend the unique role that sport can play in a develop-

ing country and the extent to which that role may differ from
the part played by sport in Western development.

This lack of sympathy and understanding has led to the
proliferation of myths and misconceptions about Soviet
sport that have become commonplace in the Western mass
media. These misconceptions preclude any real understanding of Soviet sport and, more important, they ensure
that the West learns little from Soviet experience. The following assumptions in particular would seem to merit re-
assessment.

*Communist nations, first and foremost the USSR, have the
advantage of size, unlimited funds and generous amenities as the
base of their sporting success.*

Population size can certainly be useful, although the
populations of China and India are treble and double the
size of that of the USSR respectively, yet neither country
has made its mark in world sport. And the German Democratic Republic, with its population of under seventeen
million, gained more gold medals at the 1976 Montreal
Olympics than the USA; Cuba with nine million people did
better than Britain or Italy or France – and the whole of
Latin America and the Caribbean put together.

Generous facilities for sport are a myth. Most Western
states have many more soccer pitches, swimming pools
and tennis courts per head of population than any communist country. Nor has any communist state amenities to
match those of the schools and colleges of North America.
A Soviet education minister has admitted that as many as
80 per cent of all Soviet secondary schools have no sports
grounds, 75 per cent have no gyms and 50 per cent do not
have even enough equipment for physical education lessons. If the total resources devoted to sport by both public
and private sectors in any advanced Western state are taken
into account, there can be no doubt that in advanced
economies like those of Britain, West Germany or North
America the financial resources per capita devoted to sport

are much, much greater than any communist country can afford. In economies of relative scarcity, like those of most of the communist world, priorities are food, housing, health and production.

*The communist states concentrate their resources on a privileged elite of professional athletes to the detriment of sport for all.*

It is important here to distinguish between *elitism* and *excellence*. Although (as we shall see in Chapter 7, which is devoted to soccer) some sportsmen enjoy a lifestyle beyond the reach of the common man, nonetheless there exist a number of strong official and social sanctions (for instance within the Press, trade unions, youth organizations and sports clubs) that militate against the cult of sports stars and the development of elitism in sport. On the other hand, excellence is unquestionably accepted and given every possible encouragement in all areas of human endeavour.

The communist states tend to regard talent in sport, like talent in music, art and mathematics, as meriting special attention from an early age. Talent is nurtured within the state system, not in private clubs. It is therefore free and open to all.

The official view is that sporting excellence should be complementary, even secondary, to sport for all. Indeed, there are serious reasons (see p. 3) why it is considered important to involve citizens of all ages in regular and active physical recreation. On the whole, at least in the towns, people can and do pursue the sport of their choice, using facilities free of charge. Sporting 'leaders' (the word 'stars' is deliberately avoided) are constantly urged to be models of good conduct, since their main task is said to be to attract more people into sport. As the double Olympic winner Valery Borzov has put it: 'The greatest compensation for all those agonizing training sessions, which are essential to top-class sport today, is the awareness that my records and achievements attract millions of people into active sport.'

*Contestants in the annual Pravda veterans' race. Sport is stressed as an aid to health and longevity*

And it is probably true to say that the excellence of Olga Korbut, for example, has inspired more young girls throughout the world with enthusiasm for gymnastics than any other athlete in history.

So although it would be naive to assume that all citizens of communist countries are sporting enthusiasts, it is likely that communist athletes do well in world sport not because they themselves are a privileged elite, but because the society they live in makes the widest possible provision for general participation in sport and the development of sporting skills.

*The communist states bring politics into sport, thereby flouting the 'amateur' ideal.*

Certainly, the USSR and all other communist countries have a big government-aided base to their sport. When a country decides that sport is a right and a duty, not a privilege to pay for, that sport cannot be left as the preserve of private clubs, that it should be as free and natural as the air people breathe, there has to be government intervention on a wide scale. And where there is such government involvement, such investment of public funds, there has to be public accountability. If that entails 'bringing politics into sport', then the communist nations stand guilty as charged. But in a centrally planned state in which health and education and much else are administered centrally, it would seem natural to run physical culture on the same lines. After all, in the USSR there have been no leisured classes able and willing to organize sports independently as a hobby.

This system of central planning and co-ordination has rendered the full-time professional in the Western sense an anachronism. Where the state is the ultimate employer, 'broken-time' payments present no problem, and the proficient athlete can be given the relative security of a studentship or an army commission for as long as he remains an active performer. It is then relatively easy to reintegrate him into normal working life in his trained profession. Very often the sports 'leaders' are fully utilized in the sports movement upon retirement, as coaches, organizers, teachers and researchers.

Sport and politics are, of course, intertwined everywhere. The communist states voice the suspicion that some Western commentators do not object to politics in sport unless it is left-wing politics. In fact, they say, there is no good cause for thinking that sport has less political significance in the West than in the USSR: first, because Western local and national government play a considerable part in providing facilities and, second, because the funds made available to sporting acitivity by 'private' and 'public' sources are by no means free of political import and intent.

*The communist countries take the fun out of sport and their treatment of athletes is inhumane; for example, the feminity of their girls is eroded.*

It is a myth that dedication is joyless; this deep-seated (British) idea is a product of the old aristocratic view that sport is only fun when toyed with. The sense of satisfaction and pride in self-fulfilment in sport can, in fact, be as profound as in any other field of human endeavour. Moreover, it is a simple fact that to develop talent to the full and to do well in, say, gymnastics or swimming (or music or ballet), one has to start young. Few people seriously object to a five-year-old pianist with talent spending a few hours each day practising; yet some feel that it is morally wrong for a talented five-year-old gymnast to spend an hour or so each day in the gymnasium. Excesses and one-sided development do occur (as we shall see later in this book), but they are the inevitable concomitants of dedication to developing a particular talent. And they are the exception.

There are well-meaning Western critics of Soviet sport who regret what they regard as dedication based on false ambition and its distortion of human development. But there are also critics who seem to make a virtue out of ignorance and a sensation out of dedication (when it concerns a communist country). A contemptuous tone is set by such headlines in the British Press as 'Automatons who do not laugh' (*The Times*) and 'Battery Huns' (*News of the World*), which echoed a BBC sports commentator's celebrated remark about East German athletes: 'They are all programmed from conception to the grave'; 'State Fish Farm' (*Daily Mail*), over an article about the impending marriage of the East German swimmers Kornelia Ender and Roland Matthes; and 'Russia's Broiler-Bred Athletes' (*The Guardian*) – an editorial replacement for my own 'What Can We Learn from Soviet Sport?'.

Complaints that lady gymnasts have to be 'trained to smile' or that swimmers with muscular arms and shoulders look 'unfeminine' betray a sexist attitude on the part of Western commentators. Why should a female gymnast, as serious and dedicated as a ballet dancer, be expected to smile and a male gymnast not? Why should it matter that girl swimmers may have muscular arms? Such attitudes seem to endorse the assumption that women may be expert in sport but must be beautiful and 'feminine' while displaying their skills; it elevates their looks and femininity, or alleged lack of it, above their achievement.

The Soviet Union makes no bones about the fact that it has used sport to further the emanciption of women in society generally, especially in erstwhile backward areas of the country. The physical liberation and naked limbs (even faces in Muslim areas!'), along with the competitive spirit associated with sport, has not been accepted in some areas without a struggle. It is worth reflecting that the graceful gymnasts Elvira Saadi and Nelli Kim come from a Muslim region where less than fifty years ago women were excluded from all public life and would probably have been stoned to death for appearing in public clad only in a leotard.

*Communist athletes do well because they fear that failure will be punished.*

Failure to comprehend the motivation of sportsmen from the communist world has given rise to a variety of theories, of which this is the most fanciful. But it is put forward not infrequently as a serious consideration. Writing in the penultimate issue of the now defunct *Sports World*, one of Britain's most respected sports writers explained why Hungary had been the first foreign soccer team to defeat England at home: 'As far as the Hungarians were concerned, with their state-subsidized rewards for the successful, it was really a case of finish of famish.' Leaving aside his criticism of state support ('state-subsidized rewards'), did he really believe that it was fear of starvation that induced Puskas and co. to run rings round England that day at Wembley in 1953? Such 'revelations' do harm to sport in the West, for they encourage a holier-than-thou attitude that tends to dismiss foreign success as based on unacceptable methods.

Despite the delusions of detractors, it is not fear of retribution for losing that motivates sportsmen from the communist states; otherwise more would defect. Only one prominent sportsman from the USSR has ever done so (the chess grandmaster Victor Korchnoi). There are many facets to that complex concept 'motivation', including good money, a town apartment, high prestige, a foreign car, travel abroad. In a comparatively closed society like that of the Soviet Union, foreign travel can certainly be an attractive inducement for the successful athlete. But it would be a mistake to ignore another essential element of motivation that produces a mixture of self-discipline, patience, dedication: patriotism – a genuine desire to do well for the good of one's team, one's people, one's country. Many Westerners, conditioned to see money as the stimulus to sacrifice, find this aspect of an athlete's motivation hard to understand. But in a country where a sportsman owes his success to the community rather than to a private club or institution, and where a successful athlete is rewarded and respected by the country he represents, patriotism can be a strong motivating force.

One of the most common explanations given in the West for communist success in sport is that the communist states provide few opportunities for entertainment for their youngsters, whereas the Western democracies provide a veritable cornucopia of leisure pursuits and therefore have fewer young people opting for sport. An American book on Soviet sport stated recently, 'it must be remembered that Russian children have little to distract them from becoming athletes-in-training. Luxuries such as toys and dolls, which seem to be necessities in capitalist societies, are not popular in a Communist nation.'[2] Illusions about 'luxuries such as toys and dolls' could be dispelled by a visit to Soviet children's stores, where toys and dolls are not only plentiful and popular, but are also subsidized to make them easily accessible to all. The cultural and recreational opportunities available in the USSR are in fact, extensive and often more conducive to a healthy and active life-style than the more passive, commercial entertainment in Western societies.

There are a number of other, even less charitable, comments on communist sport which are undeserving of serious consideration. What they all have in common is that they seek the 'secret' of communist success in sport in peripheral elements and exaggerated (sensationalized) generalities, *not in the sports system itself.*

Such uniformed comment regularly takes the place of serious study and comparative assessment; it does not help us to understand communist sport or to learn any lessons ourselves. It would seem logical to suggest that a sports specialist can only gain access to a foreign culture, and therefore to its sports system, by reading and conversing in that foreign tongue. A foreign language is obligatory for every student of physical education and every student-coach in the USSR; moreover, not only are many foreign sports books regularly translated into Russian, but a monthly journal, *Sport za rubezhom* (*Sport Abroad*), consists entirely of information about foreign sport. Significantly, the debut of Soviet athletes in the the Olympics and world championships in the early 1950s was prefaced by a careful study of the attainments of Western sport, of training methods and tactical skills. Soviet scholars tried to learn all they could from the West, to emulate and adapt the positive features of Western sport. Since then they have kept up their diligent study of Western research into sport and physical education, and they have incorporated all that is valuable and suitable into their own system, thereby obviating unnecessary duplication in research.

In sharp contrast, virtually no study is made in the West of Soviet sport – arguably the most successful system in the world in terms of Olympic and world Championship performances. Remarkably, at least until the early 1970s no library in North America, including those in schools of physical education and faculties of medicine, subscribed to the leading Soviet journal on sport and physical education *Teoriya i praktika fizicheskoi kul'tury* (*Theory and Practice of Physical Culture*). Ignorance of foreign sport is not confined to that of the USSR. In English-speaking countries hardly any students of physical education, and even fewer coaches, have an adequate knowledge of a foreign language. Though we in the West fondly imagine that all foreigners can speak English, they do not translate their specialist knowledge and experience into English for our benefit. In consequence, we are often fed with ill-informed and frequently malicious 'explanations' of Soviet sporting success.

In this book I an concerned to define and explain the main differences between the Soviet sport system and those of the West. But the reader should not lose sight of some essentially human characteristics which are likely to be common to most sports systems. It would seem that in an urban civilization, with its increasing preponderance of sedentary occupations, sport is regarded as a necessary means of maintaining physical fitness. Where many take part, some will be better than others and will want to strive for the highest attainments. The incentives that motivate individuals in a relentless and dedicated pursuit of excellence will be as varied as the individuals themselves. And this is no less true of sportsmen in the Soviet Union. However, the view taken by the Soviet sports authorities, and in the other communist countries generally, is that sporting success should not depend solely on the physical and moral resources of the individual participant, as it so often does in the West, but should be instead the result of the co-ordinated effort of the total sports system. Success is a measure of the effectiveness with which the resources of the entire society can be brought to bear on the encouragement of participation at all levels and on the development of talents of all kinds.

## NOTES

[1] Y. D. Kotov, I. I. Yudovich, *Sovetskaya shakhmatnaya shkola* (Moscow, 1951), p. 4.
[2] N. Maclean, B. Wilner, E. Hoerner, *Soviet Sport Exercise Program* (New York, 1977), pp. 19–20.

Chapter 2

# *The Evolution of the Sports System*

When the Bolsheviks took power in October 1917 they found the country in chaos and ruin. It was on this foundation that the 'brave new world' of communist sport had to be constructed. The first steps to be taken were by no means clear, for there was no pattern to follow: the change-over from criticism of tsarist sport to action in a largely peasant country in the throes of a world and civil war presented enormous problems.

However, the crucial question under debate in those early years was not what form sport should take, but *whether there was any place at all for competitive sport* in the new workers' state. After all, some revolutionaries argued, field and track events, soccer, rowing, tennis, and gymnastics were almost entirely invented by the bourgeoisie for its own diversion and as character training for future captains of industry and empire. Just as during the Renaissance the emergent ruling class had developed a substantially new pattern of sport imbued with their own values, usurping the more casual field sports of the feudal aristocracy, so it was thought perfectly natural by some that a new pattern of recreation should emerge after the Russian Revolution, reflecting the workers' needs in the new socialist state.

*The Post-Revolutionary Years*

Essentially, sport during the first few years after the Revolution was geared to the needs of the war effort. All the old clubs and their equipment were commandeered and handed over to Vsevobuch, the new military training establishment, whose main aim was to supply the Red Army with contingents of trained conscripts as quickly as possible. One means of achieving this was to carry out a crash programme designed to promote physical fitness in all people of recruitable age.

In line with the policy of combining military drill and weapon-handling with political and general education in elementary hygiene, it was also decided that the activities of Vsevobuch should be co-ordinated with those of the commissariats of education and health. In the opinion of the head of Vsevobuch, Nikolai Podvoisky, it was impossible to bring the civil war to a successful conclusion, or even to build socialism, without the support of a large-scale campaign to improve physical fitness and health.

A second major consideration, then, was health. Having inherited a country with an inclement climate, where disease and starvation were common and where most people had only a rudimentary knowledge of hygiene, the Soviet leaders acknowledged that it would take a radical economic and social transformation to alter the situation substantially. But time was short, and able-bodied and disciplined men and women were vital, first for the country's survival, then for its recovery from the ravages of war and revolution, its industrial development and its defence against further attacks.

Regular participation in physical exercise was to be one means – a relatively inexpensive but effective one – of improving health standards rapidly and a channel by which to educate people in hygiene, nutrition and exercise. One indication of the kind of health policy that was adopted is the campaign mounted during the civil war under the slogans 'Help the Country with a Toothbrush!', 'Help the Country by Washing in Cold water!' and 'Physical Culture 24 Hours a Day!'. With the influx into the cities of masses of peasants who brought with them rural habits, the drive to inculcate the principles of health and hygiene through physical exercise took on a new urgency. The ignorance that was the cause of so much disease, starvation and misery – and that hampered both military effectiveness and labour productivity – was to be combated by a broad programme of physical exercise and sport. And if material facilities were lacking, then people were urged to make full use of 'the sun, air, water and natural movement – the best proletarian doctors'.

The campaign could only catch on, in Podvoisky's opinion, if the emotional attraction of competitive sport were exploited to the utmost – and this at a time when 'competition' and 'sport' had become rather dirty words; certainly, a number of educationalists regarded competitive sports as debasing physical culture and inculcating non-socialist habits. The two major groups that led the attack on sport were the Hygienists and the Proletkultists.

To the Hygienists, sport implied competition, games that were potentially injurious to mental and physical health. Such pursuits as boxing, weightlifting, wrestling, even gymnastics, were said to be irrational and dangerous and to encourage individualist rather than collectivist attitudes. They frowned upon the record-breaking mania of contemporary sport in the West and favoured non-commercialized forms of recreation that dispensed with grandstands and spectators. Sport, they averred, diverted attention from the need to provide recreation for all; it turned the masses into onlookers. The list of 'approved' sports included field and track events, swimming and rowing, where sportsmen competed against themselves or the clock, not against opponents; 'non-approved' sports included boxing, wrestling, soccer and fencing, all of which involved competition with others. At the same time the Hygienists managed to exclude physical education from the schools, since they believed it should be incorporated into all lessons and not tacked on to the curriculum artificially. During the 1920s the Hygienists had virtual control over the government body for sport (the Supreme Council of Physical Culture), the sporting Press, the Health Ministry and the physical education colleges.

To the Proletkultists, sports that derived from bourgeois society were remnants of the decadent past and part of degenerate bourgeois culture. A fresh start had to be made through labour exercises and mass displays, pageants and folk games. Sports equipment and gymnasiums had to be replaced by workaday pieces of apparatus on which workers and peasants could practise their labour movements. Thus, in the decade after the Revolution, many factory yards and fields could be seen full of muscular men and women rhythmically swinging hammers and sickles, simulating work movements. The Proletkultists went much further than the Hygienists in condemning all manner of games, sports and gymnastics 'tainted' by bourgeois society. They invented new games for children and mass 'sports' activities, such as 'A Pageant of Universal October', portraying scenes of world revolution, and 'Indians, British and Reds' – the latter taking place on Moscow's Sparrow Hills in the summer of 1924, with over 6000 participants. While the Hygienists admitted the possibility of using some 'bourgeois' sports, the Proletkultists made no such concession. They condemned tennis, for example, as fit only for the bourgeois 'white-pants' brigade. It exhibited no comradeship and was unsuitable for proletarians. Several other sports were banned; the First Trade Union Games, in 1925, for example, outlawed boxing, soccer, gymnastics and weightlifting.

Nonetheless, competitive sports and contests began to

be organized from the lowest level upwards, culminating in the All-Russia Pre-Olympiads and the First Central Asian Olympics of 1920. Sports were taken from the town to the countryside, from the European metropolis to the Asiatic interior, as an explicit means of involving as many people as possible in organized sport and physical exercise. As the health minister, Nikolai Semashko, put it:

Sport is the open gate to physical culture. It not only fortifies the various organs of the body, it aids mental development, teaches attentiveness, punctuality and precision of movement; it develops will power, strength and skill – the very virtues that should distinguish Soviet people.

A third function of sport was integration. The significance of the First Central Asian Olympics, held in the old Islamic centre, Tashkent, over a period of ten days in early October 1920, may be judged from the fact that this was the first time in history that Uzbeks, Kazakhs, Turkmenians, Kirgiz and other Turkic peoples, as well as Russians and other Europeans, had competed in any sporting event together. Integrative policies aside, these sporting initiatives should be seen as a highly principled aspect of the general cultural emancipation of what were formerly subject peoples.

Thus, at the dawn of the Soviet state three ingredients in the sports policy were made explicit by the new regime – health, defence and integration.

It was during the 1920s that the Party clarified its views on physical culture and took it completely under government control. In its famous resolution of 1925 the Party stressed that

physical culture must be considered not simply from the standpoint of public health and physical education, not only as an aspect of the cultural, economic and military training of young people. It should also be seen as a means to educate the masses (inasmuch as it develops will power, teamwork, endurance,

*Popular folk sport of* kyzz-koo *in Central Asia: a male rider chases (and catches) a female rider*

resourcefulness and other valuable qualities). It must be regarded, moreover, as a means of rallying the bulk of the workers and peasants to the various Party, government and trade-union organizations, through which they can be drawn into social and political activity . . . Physical culture must be an inseparable part of overall political and cultural education and of public health.

This, then, was the definitive statement on the role of sport in society to which all subsequent policy statements were to refer. We have already seen that sport was employed as a means of inculcating standards of hygiene and regular exercise in a predominantly backward peasant country; its therapeutic value was, for example, widely advertised in the intermittent three-day anti-tuberculosis campaigns of the late 1920s. It was also not considered incongruous to distribute a poster ostensibly advertising sports, yet featuring a young man with a rifle and toothbrush above the slogan 'Clean Your Teeth! Clean Your Rifle!' (presumably not with the toothbrush!)

But sport was not confined to improving physical health; it was regarded as important in combating anti-social behaviour in town and country. If young people, especially those in towns, could be persuaded to take up sport and engage in regular physical exercise, they might develop healthy bodies *and* minds. Thus the Ukrainian Party Central Committee issued a resolution in 1926 expressing the hope that

physical culture would become the vehicle of the new life . . . a means of isolating young people from the evil influence of the street, home-made liquor and prostitution.

The role assigned to sport in the countryside was even more ambitious: it was

to play a big part in the campaign against drunkenness and uncivilized behaviour by attracting village youth to more sensible and cultured activities . . . In the fight to transform the village, physical culture is to be a vehicle of the new way of life in all measures undertaken by the Soviet authorities – in the fight against religion and natural calamities.

Sport, then, stood for 'clean living', progress, good health and rationality, and it was regarded by the Party as one of the most suitable and effective instruments for implementing its social policies.

## *Sport against the Background of Industrialization*

By the end of the 1920s the scene was set for the implementation of an industrialization programme that was to hurl the whole of the country into a gigantic effort to 'build socialism', to lead to the forcible collectivization of agriculture and to transform the USSR from a backward agrarian into an advanced industrial economy – all on the nation's own resources.

The implications for the sports movement of these economic processes were extremely important, for it was in the 1930s that the pattern of Soviet sport as we know it today was formed and its main role and functions determined. By the end of the 1930s the basic organizational pattern had already been established – with its sports societies, sports schools, national fitness programme – '*Gotov k trudu i oborone*' (GTO): 'Ready for Labour and Defence' – and uniform rankings system for individual sports and proficient athletes. The Soviet society of the 1930s differed from that of the preceding period in that it saw the expansion of all manner of competitive sports (soccer, basketball, volleyball) with mass spectator appeal, and the official encouragement of leagues, stadiums, cups, championships, popularity polls, cults of sporting heroes – all the appendages, in fact, of a system designed to provide general recreation and diversion for the fast-growing urban populace.

Millions of people, uprooted from centuries-old traditions, were pitched into new and strange environments; newcomers to industry joined factory clubs and looked to them for the recreation they had previously enjoyed in an open-air, rural setting. Urban conditions were spartan and deteriorating (in 1926 the average housing space per person had only been 8.2 square metres and by 1940 it was down to 6.4 square metres). Sports therefore served many towns-folk as an escape from the drudgery of their domestic and work environments. The many sports parades and pageants which constituted a background to the sports contests of the 1930s were intended, too, to create and reinforce a sense of 'togetherness', to evoke feelings of patriotism and to demonstrate to people at home as well as abroad how happy and carefree life was under socialism. It is significant that sports rallies often accompanied major political events or festivals (May Day, the anniversary of the October Revolution, Constitution Day). In this way, sport became a means of linking members of the public with politics, the Party and, of course, their leader.

*Cycling race through the streets of Moscow. This is an urban sport only recently made popular with the advent of mass cycle production*

Further, a relatively close link was re-established in the 1930s between sport and the military. It stemmed from the conviction that a state surrounded by unfriendly powers needed to be militarily strong and constantly on the alert. This conviction became widespread in the 'besieged fortress' atmosphere of the 1930s and was encouraged by the rise of Fascism in Europe. Sport openly became a means of providing pre-military training and of achieving a relatively high standard of national fitness and defence.

Several sports with potential military application – for instance, shooting, gliding, skiing and mountaineering – came to be dominated by servicemen. The two largest and most successful sports clubs in the USSR were those run by the armed forces and the security forces: the Central House of the Red Army (today the Central Sports Club of the Army, TsSKA) and Dinamo respectively. And after 1931 the GTO national fitness programme was expressly intended to train people, through sport, for work and military preparedness.

## World War II

The war years should not be regarded as a wasted interlude that retarded the sports movement. They had certain consequences, some intangible but nonetheless far-reaching, whose effect was evident for many years.

The war convinced the Soviet leadership that it had been right to 'functionalize' sport and make countrywide physical fitness a prime target. It also reinforced a belief in a military bias in physical training and sport. After the war the role of military organizations like the army sports clubs, Dinamo and the civil defence organization DOSAAF was to be enhanced, and these institutions were to form the pillars of the whole sports movement. A national physical-fitness programme was to be the principal goal, and sports with specific military utility were to become compulsory in all educational institutions and sports societies.

Victory in the war also gave the Soviet people a sense of pride in their achievements, a feeling that the period of pre-war industrialization and sacrifice had been justified.

Now they could take on the world in another (peaceful) form of contest, sport, one in which they could test their potential. But the war had been won at a price: the awful fact emerged that over twenty million Soviet men, women and children had lost their lives. And many Soviet people felt that they had borne the brunt of German might and had made untold sacrifices to free the world from the blight of Fascism. The resultant feelings of patriotism were to be an evident part of the motivation for seeking victory in international sports competitions.

*Post-War Developments*

With the conclusion of the war and the setting of a new national target – that of catching up and overtaking the most advanced industrial powers (and that included catching up and overtaking in sport too) – the Soviet leadership felt it possible to demonstrate the pre-eminence of sport in socialist society. Given the limited opportunities elsewhere, sport seemed to offer a suitable medium for pursuing this goal; this was an area in which the USSR did not have to take second place to the West. And as we shall see below, since the war the Soviet Union has gone a considerable way to achieving this target. Of course, this policy presupposed a level of skill in a wide range of sports superior to that existing in the leading Western states. On the eve of the war Soviet sport was already approaching that level in several sports; in some it had actually reached it. This trend was strengthened after the war by the mobilization of the total (if limited) resources of the entire sports system and by the creation and whole-hearted support of full-time, well remunerated sportsmen and teams.

Another factor of paramount importance to the post-war development of sport has been the qualitative change in urban life and leisure. Since the late 1950s particularly, there has been a fairly steady increase in public and personal prosperity, a marked growth in the range and quantity of consumer goods available, a reduction in working time and a continuing shift in population balance in favour of the towns (the urban population first exceeded the rural in 1961). All these factors are having a qualitative effect on the pattern of sport.

### INCREASING PROSPERITY

Figures published in the USSR indicate that both national income and consumption have more than doubled since 1960. Thus total national income increased from 145 to 338 million rubles between 1960 and 1973; of that sum, the

*Recently constructed Olympic rowing course in Moscow*

amount accounted for by personal consumption rose from 104 to 224 million rubles. Part of the increased personal income is undoubtedly being spent on recreation and sport, on the pursuit of a growing variety of activities, particularly outdoor ones, and on consumer durables such as skis, skates, tennis and badminton rackets, fishing tackle, tents and, to a lesser extent, motor cycles, canoes, dinghies, yachts and cars (it is estimated that by 1980–5 the USSR will have between fifteen and twenty million passenger cars, that is, approximately one for every four or five families). This is clearly a long-term trend. Higher national income has also resulted in the allocation of more substantial government funds to sports facilities and the development of a number of activities that presuppose a certain level of industrial development and economic surplus. For example, motor racing and rallying, yachting, karting, various winter sports (tobogganing, bobsleighing, slaloming, ski-jumping), water-skiing, aqualung diving, mountaineering, fishing, shooting and the complex of activities that come under the rubric of 'tourism' all showed appreciable growth in the 1960s and 1970s. Some sports received a new lease of life as industry was able to produce equipment for them – as, for example, in the cases of rugby, archery and field hockey. The most recently introduced sports for which facilities are at present being constructed are squash, karate, hang-gliding and golf.

INCREASING FREE TIME

The relationship of work and leisure has also altered radically in the last two decades. Not only has there been an increase in the amount of leisure time, but the reduction in the working day has resulted in workers spending less time than before in such institutional settings as factory and office. The breakthrough that signalled the greatest revolution in the pattern of recreation, just as in other advanced industrial countries, was the introduction of the long weekend in March 1967. The boom in camping, fishing, hunting, rock climbing, pot-holing, water-skiing, motoring and boating is partly accounted for by longer holidays with pay and partly by the developing cult of the weekend. In 1956 the standard (6 day) week in Soviet industry was 46 hours; by 1961 it had declined to 41 hours (still in a 6-day week) – that is, most workers had 5 7-hour days and 1 6-hour day each week. In 1970 the average working week in industry was 40.7 hours and, in state employment in general, 39.4 hours in a 5-day week. Altogether, Soviet industrial manual workers had 95.4 days off during 1974, including paid annual holidays of 15 days for most workers.

INCREASING URBANIZATION

Over half the Soviet population now lives in a relatively modern, urban, industrial society. Whereas only 18 per cent of the population lived in towns in 1926, today over 60 per cent is urban-based – that is, 156 million people in a population exceeding 260 million. Furthermore, the USSR has eleven cities with populations exceeding a million and thirty-five cities of over half a million. This is a condition which, in itself and regardless of political activities, predisposes people to certain kinds of recreational activities. As people have migrated to the towns, the government has followed a policy of high-density building. Despite the fact that in the USSR town planning tends to allow for sizeable courtyards for each multi-storey block of flats, the problem of providing adequate outdoor amenities for sport is becoming ever greater in the most densely settled urban areas.

Thus, since the war rising personal prosperity, an increasing amount of free time, particularly the long weekend, and the pressures of an urban–industrial environment have had certain implications for sport. For

*May Day in Red Square. Sports parades are invariably a feature of major political festivals*

example, people are tending to form smaller (family) groups for recreation and holidays. There appears to be an increasing desire to 'get away from it all' rather than to 'get together'. In the past the leadership generally tried to see to it that the amenities available to the community inclined citizens towards some form of public, collective recreation – mainly through the sports club, the workplace, the trade union, the public park or the play centre behind a block of flats. Now that most workers have a long weekend away from work, these production-based facilities no longer seem to suit them. The trend, therefore, is for the public to reject 'public and mass' sports activities in favour of individual, domestic, family and passive leisure pursuits.

One problem that has been taxing the authorities increasingly is the task of ensuring that this additional free time is used in a rational way – that leisure is socially functional. Time spent on sporting activities is held to be valuable because of the contribution sport makes to production and the smooth functioning of society in general. Sport enriches the individual, and he in turn enriches society. Nonetheless, a whole range of activities that appear to be at variance with notions of rationality are tolerated. One such activity is horse racing as a spectator sport for gamblers. Horse racing – flat racing, steeplechasing, hurdle and trotting races – is, in fact, regarded as the only fully professional sport in the USSR and is extremely popular, attracting more spectators even than soccer. The Moscow Hippodrome racecourse, for example, is open three times a week all the year round and draws an average crowd of 13,000 on a Sunday. Punters may place a bet of up to ten rubles on any race (for a win, a double, or first or second place) through the state totalizator. Three-quarters of the receipts are paid out in winnings.

Other sporting activities, however, have been attacked – sometimes even proscribed – because of their alleged 'irrationality' or exhibitionism, or because they have lent themselves to commercial exploitation. Such activities include women's soccer and wrestling, male body-building, yoga, karate and bridge – all of which were censured in a government resolution of January 1973 (although karate has since been rehabilitated).

At the same time, with more money, more free time and a wider range of recreational pursuits to choose from, Soviet people are today increasingly able to select the sporting activity that most accords with their own talents and inclinations. As facilities and opportunities improve, participation in sport is governed less by the official utilitarian approach and more by the idea that a game, a sport or an outdoor activity of any kind is desirable for its own sake.

Chapter 3

# The Structure and Organization of Soviet Sport

The administration of sport came under the aegis of the state right after the Revolution, and the sports movement has since been fully integrated with the political system. Sport and politics in the USSR are therefore inseparable and, as we have seen, sport has been used over the Soviet period as a means to achieving specific socio-political ends.

Overall direction of the sports movement is today provided by the USSR Committee on Physical Culture and Sport, which is attached to the USSR Council of Ministers (the central government). Its chairman is Sergei Pavlov, one-time Secretary of the Communist Youth League (the Komsomol). The USSR Sports Committee is the umbrella organization for all other elements of the sports movement: the individual sports federations, the various sports societies, sports schools, coaching, research, competition, medicine, etc. (see Fig. 1).

Actual organization is in the hands of thirty-six sports societies, all but two of which are run by the trade unions, including fifteen urban Republican societies, fifteen rural Republican and four All-Union (Burevestnik representing students, Lokomotiv representing railwaymen, Vodnik representing river transport employees and Spartak repre-

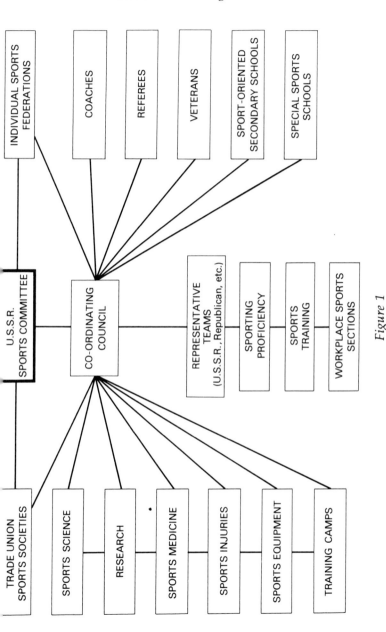

*Figure 1*

*The administrative structure of sports in the USSR*

senting 'white-collar workers'). The two non-trade-union societies are Dinamo and Labour Reserves, the former run by the Ministry for Internal Security and the latter representing students at technical colleges. (Dinamo is also the biggest manufacturer of sports equipment in the country, operating over fifty plants and many retail sports shops. Most of the twenty million rubles Dinamo spent on sport in 1975 were taken from its business enterprises.) The one major sports organization outside this framework is the Central Army Sports Club.

Each society has its own rules, membership cards, badge and colours. The societies are financed out of trade union dues (a 1 per cent levy on each union member; a quarter of trade-union funds go to sport) and given responsibility for building sports centres, acquiring equipment for their members and maintaining permanent staffs of coaches, instructors and medical personnel. All members have the right to use the Societies' facilities for a nominal fee of 30 kopecks a year and to elect and be elected to their managing committees.

Contests are organized between sports societies and clubs. Each society has its own local and nationwide championships for each sport it practises, and its teams play against teams representing other societies. There therefore exist nationwide sports leagues and cup competitions in a whole range of popular sports, such as soccer, ice hockey, basketball and volleyball. All the trade-union sports societies have 'teams of masters' in every major town, as do the sports clubs of the armed services and Dinamo. The trade unions are thus directly responsible for organizing competitions both within their own sports societies and on a nationwide basis, including in the *spartakiads*, which are modelled on the Olympic programme and are now held in the two years preceding each Olympic Games. One of the major problems in organizing competitive sport in the West is the cost of moving teams about the country. In a centrally run country like the USSR, even though the land is so vast, this is much less of a problem, teams and individual athletes being given free travel passes (like servicemen), which are issued by their club on behalf of the government.

The two interlinked elements that underlie the whole sports system are the GTO mass fitness programme and the uniform rankings system for individual sports. Both were instituted in the early 1930s and both were intended to serve the twin aims of *massovost* (mass participation) and *masterstvo* (proficiency). While the GTO sets targets for all-round ability in a number of sports and knowledge of the rudiments of hygiene and first aid (for which token gold and silver badges are awarded), the rankings system contains a whole set of qualifying standards, rankings and titles in individual sports, intended to stimulate the best performers to aim for certain graduated standards (see Fig. 2).

*The GTO Programme*

It is through the GTO that most Soviet people take part in sport, and the programme is regarded as the foundation of the sports system. The target is not excellence in a single sport, nor even general skills, but all-round ability in a number of events and knowledge of hygiene, first aid and sports theory. The programme has five stages, determined by age, which all necessitate a certain minimum performance in running, jumping, throwing, shooting, skiing and gymnastics. The programme (which is revised every ten years on average) set in March 1972 had the following five stages:

(a) boys and girls aged 10–13;
(b) boys and girls aged 14–15;
(c) Boys and girls aged 16–18 (see Appendix 1);

(d) women aged 19–34, men aged 19–39;
(e) women aged 35–55, men aged 40–60 (older people may compete only with a doctor's permission).

GTO planning quotas are set for every club, society, region and school, and tests are held throughout the year. The main concern of most sports clubs is, in fact, to see that their members obtain their GTO badges. There seems little doubt that most young people are caught up in this fitness campaign: in the decade 1970–80 it is estimated that an average of eighteen million people qualified for a GTO badge every year.

The GTO has as its stated aim to make regular participation in sport a permanent feature of the Soviet way of life. More specifically, the motives behind the programme would seem to include the following. First, to attract children into sport at an early age, partly because it is felt that the earlier they become engaged in sport and keeping fit, the more likelihood there is of their taking part in sporting activity later on, and partly because to achieve international success in many sports, it is increasingly necessary to spot talent and develop it at an early age. Second, the GTO is used for direct military training: a civil defence test and gas mask training are to be found at every stage, and rifle shooting at three stages. The element of military preparation is especially evident in the programme for the 16–18 age group, many of whose members will be entering the armed forces with some training (through the GTO) behind them. Third, an often stated reason for drawing people into the fitness campaign is to cut down absenteeism from work through illness by making workers physically and mentally more alert (through sport) to cope with the changing techniques of industry – and thereby raising productivity. Fourth, the GTO would appear to be important as an attempt to channel the zest and energy of young people into relatively healthy recreation. In a speech inaugurating the new GTO programme in 1972, the sports

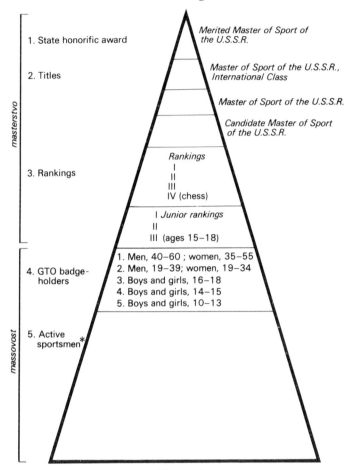

*Figure 2*
*Sport titles and rankings pyramid*

* Active sportsmen are officially defined as members of sports groups who engage in sport under the supervision of an instructor not less than twice a week over a minimum period of six months. In 1978, the number was put by the Chairman of the Sports Committee at Sixty million people – that is, over one-fifth of the population. By contrast, however, several surveys have indicated one-tenth of the population as a more realistic estimate – that is, twenty-six million.

minister, Pavlov, made most of these points: 'The GTO must be used to organize people's leisure more rationally, to improve public health and prevent industrial disease, to combat misuse of increasing leisure time, to tighten up labour and public discipline, and to improve educative work among young people.'

## The Sports Rankings System

This system is intended to stimulate the best athletes to aim for certain set standards in a particular sport and to help coaches to select promising sportsmen to train with specific targets in mind. A whole complex of qualifying standards, rankings and titles exist for the eighty officially registered sports. These are updated every four years on average, to coincide with the Olympic cycle.

The two top titles (Master of Sport of the USSR, International Class, and Master of Sport of the USSR) are honorary and are conferred for life. The only higher award to which an outstanding and internationally successful athlete may aspire is Merited Master of Sport of the USSR, but this is a state honorific decoration outside the classification system (like Merited Artist or Merited Teacher of the USSR). In chess and draughts the title Grand Master of the USSR is the equivalent of Master of Sport of the USSR, International Class, for other sports. In addition, the title Master of Folk Sport exists for a variety of folk games and sports.

Besides these titles and decorations, the top Soviet sportsmen, coaches and officials are regularly included in the country's 'honours list'. After the Montreal Olympic Games in 1976, for example, a total of 347 Olympic athletes, coaches and officials received awards, ranging from the supreme honour – the Order of Lenin – to the Order of the Red Banner of Labour. The recipients of the Order of Lenin were four athletes: Ludmilla Turishcheva, Nikolai Andrianov, Levan Tediashvili and Ivan Yarygin (two gymnasts and two wrestlers); three coaches and the sports minister, Sergei Pavlov.

The two top titles mentioned above are awarded mainly on the basis of international success, but an athlete must first meet all the rankings standards for his sport. Sports rankings 1–3 are awarded for results achieved in official Soviet competition (All-Union championships, *spartakiads*, cups, and so on) and are valid for one or two years only, after which they either lapse or have to be renewed – or, of course, the athlete may try for a higher ranking. To obtain a second or third ranking, the athlete must also have satisfied the requirements of the GTO programme for his particular age category. The qualifying standards for each category are high and are revised regularly to keep pace with changing world standards.

In some sports (for example, swimming and running) the athlete competes against the clock; in others the rankings may depend on the number of victories gained in contests with athletes of equivalent or higher rankings. In boxing, for example, the 1977–80 classifications stipulated that to become a Master of Sport, International Class, the contender had to be among the first eight in the Olympics or World Championships, or among the first three in the European Championships. To gain a second adult ranking, a boxer must have eight victories in a year against third-ranking boxers. Each ranking has to be renewed every year by gaining three victories over boxers of the same ranking or six wins over boxers in the ranking immediately below. In team games victories in regular league and cup games count. For example, for the third basketball ranking a player must be a member of a team that has won no fewer than seven matches during a year against teams of any qualification in a national league, as long as the player has made at least fourteen appearances for the team.

Junior rankings are awarded to athletes under 18 years of age who have also met the qualifying standards of the appropriate GTO programme for their age.

A badge and a certificate are awarded by the USSR Sports Committee for each title, plus a financial award (thirty rubles a month in the case of a Master of Sport – that is, about one-fifth of the average Soviet monthly industrial earnings). Ranked sportsmen also receive a badge from the sports society to which they belong. All such athletes have the right to take part in official competitions and their applications for admission to sports schools and colleges of physical education are given preferential treatment. Along with these rights, however, go certain duties: to conduct oneself in accordance with sporting ethics; to pass on one's expertise and experience to others; to compete on behalf of one's group or club; to improve one's political and cultural standards; constantly to submit to medical supervision.

Any violation of these obligations may result in the loss of the ranking or title – a not infrequent occurence. In soccer, as we shall see below, several players have been deprived of their awards in recent years for receiving under-cover payments, or for behaving badly in public or during matches. Leading athletes are expected to be models of good behaviour at all times.

To sum up, the two systems, the GTO programme and the rankings system, are intended to operate together so that general interest in sport is sustained from school onwards, and so that as little potential talent as possible is wasted. In a country as vast as the USSR, they are a means of establishing standardization and yardsticks for measuring progress in the proficient and deficient areas of Soviet sport.

# Chapter 4

# *Talent*

Talent is a much debated quality. In societies where consideration is given to the bright rather than to the dim, to the gifted few rather than to the average many, to those with means rather than to those without, it is natural that there should be a healthy scepticism about so-called talent. It is not easy to get the balance right, especially in an economy of relative scarcity, between the amount of attention paid to the average and that devoted to the above average (or even the below average). Nor is it easy to make the one complementary to the other. It is not obvious, even less generally accepted, what talent is, how to find it or what to do with it once it has been discovered. Not everyone would agree that sporting talent should be treated in the same way as artistic and intellectual giftedness.

Controversies apart – and they are equally fierce in the communist world – it does seem to be accepted that the Soviet Union and some other communist nations, most notably Cuba and the German Democratic Republic, are reasonably successful in spotting and developing talent in sport, as in ballet, music and mathematics.

In the official Soviet view, the principle of sport for all has always taken precedence over the training of the talented few. And it would be wrong to imagine that scarce resources are lavished upon the gifted minority to the deprivation of the mediocre masses. But ever since the late 1920s 'leaders' in ever walk of life have been valued highly in Soviet society – whether they have been exemplary coal miners, scientists or sportsmen. There would seem to be three main reasons why the USSR displays such concern for its gifted athletes, its potential sports leaders.

First, sportsmen are held in high esteem for the skill, grace and strength by which they inspire young and old alike to be active and to join in at all levels of sport. They also help to instil a pride in one's team, nationality and country, and even in the political system that can produce such world-beaters. The conduct of sports personalities is therefore expected to be exemplary, an inspiration to all.

Second, Soviet sport follows foreign policy and has important functions to discharge. These functions include winning support for the USSR and its policies among developing nations; maintaining and reinforcing the unity of the socialist countries; gaining recognition and prestige in the world generally; and, most important of all, demonstrating the advantages of the communist way of life. As a consequence, besides winning World Championships and Olympic medals, talented Soviet athletes are expected to be ambassadors of good will and models of propriety in the arenas and forums of the world.

Third, there is a strong belief in the USSR in the parity of mental and physical culture in human development, and a conviction that talent in sport should be treated no differently from talent in art, music or science. In other words, budding gymnasts, say, should be regarded in the same way as promising ballet dancers: they must be given every opportunity to develop their gifts. Furthermore, unlike the early administrators of amateur sport in the West, the Soviet leadership has never been constrained by the notion that sport is an unworthy profession or career.

Given this philosophy, it is logical that the USSR should have an extensive screening system in schools and in clubs designed to sift out talent at an early age. In some sports where talent blossoms early, as in swimming and gymnastics, this may mean starting as young as 5 or 6. Children with natural ability are therefore brought together in a well-equipped environment, given special and intensive coaching and tested regularly by medical personnel. They are given every chance to become proficient, to gain a sports ranking and to graduate to one of the country's top teams or squads. All such schools for talent are free.

## Finding and Developing Talent

The Soviet education system is comprehensive and co-educational; its philosophy lays emphasis on the importance of environment as against heredity, and on hard work and staying power as against innate ability. Given the right environment and opportunity, it is thought, all children are educable and can, with profit, follow the same school classes from 7 to 17. The accent is on co-operation rather than competition. There are no private, independent or semi-independent schools; but the USSR does have a small number of residential schools for the handicapped and for children talented in art, music, ballet, mathematics and sport. All the same, Soviet educationalists regard heredity as a vital element in the formation of personality and physical traits. Their view is that talent is a rare, inborn quality, which a suitable environment can discover, nurture and harness to the common good. The most common phenomenon, however, is average ability; giftedness, like complete mediocrity, occurs infrequently. This approach has important implications for the selection of methods of seeking and developing talent. Even an increase in special residential schools, for example, would only ensure an increase in average results. Hence the importance accorded to spotting talent, encouraging its emergence and giving it every chance to come to fruition.

Talented individuals are thought to possess the following basic qualities: abounding physical energy, a capacity for hard work, specific qualities of mind and character and an inner stimulus. But talent is generally a specialized faculty; to be gifted in one way does not imply all-round ability. What is vital in sport is the possession of qualities that are needed for specific activities: an explosive take-off in the high jump, a combination of speed and strength of thrust in the long jump, oxygen intake and stamina in long-distance running, skiing, rowing and swimming. All these attributes are believed to be inborn and capable of refinement by rational training.

There is no place here to examine how talent is spotted and tested for its future potential. Obviously, the methods used vary according to the demands of each particular sport. Suffice it to say that tests are normally extensive and cover such elements as respiratory capacity, muscle tissue, blood and urine, proportionate development of muscles and body parts (finger size, forearm, neck, calf and so on).

The spotting and the nurturing of talent are aided considerably by the concerted efforts of all branches of the state system, in particular the research institutes and sports medicine. It is the task of the physical education research institutes, for example, to develop special testing devices to measure potential talent, to develop new training methods and equipment for the top teams (and even individual athletes) to compile textbooks and manuals and to publish learned articles on sport. They were instrumental, for example, in discovering the 'right' partner for the champion figure skater Irina Rodnina after the departure of her previous partner Ulyanov. It came as a surprise to some in the West that a relatively unknown, inexperienced and slightly built young man, Alexander Zaitsev, was chosen out of several hundred candidates who underwent many months of thorough testing. Yet the pair became the most successful figure skaters in the sport, ideally suited both in physical skills and psychological temperament (to the

*Irina Rodnina and her husband Alexei Zaitsev, long-reigning world pairs figure-skating champions*

extent, even, of becoming marriage partners). Another example of intensive research applied to talent-spotting was the discovery of the sprinter Valery Borzov. Once again, he was found after extensive tests among literally hundreds of promising sprinters. His subsequent success as the first Soviet athlete to win both the 100 metres and the 200 metres at the 1972 Olympics was rightly regarded as vindication of the meticulous research methods. It is worthy of note that in the twilight of his active race career Borzov himself is a postgraduate student at the Kiev Physical Culture Institute and is writing a dissertation (1979) on 'Starting Techniques in Sprinting'; his coach, Dr V. V. Petrovsky, is a Candidate of Biological Science and author of several scientific treatises. As other examples of sportsmen who hold scientific qualifications, Anatoly Tarasov, former long-serving senior coach to the all-conquering Soviet ice hockey squad and the Central Army Sports Club, is the author of books on ice hockey techniques and a Candidate of Science; the former USSR athletics team coach Gavril Korobkov is an eminent engineer; Vladimir Dyachkov, coach to high jumper Valery Brumel, is a biomechanics specialist and author of a 400-page manual on high-jumping techniques; former boxer Valery Popenchenko (holder of the Barker trophy as best boxer at the 1964 Olympic Games) became a Candidate of Technical Sciences and the faculty head at Moscow's Institute of Technology. There are, in fact, few coaches and team officials associated with Soviet representative teams who are not qualified specialists, professionally trained in science and medicine and employed in sport according to their particular specialism.


*Medical Supervision*

Medical supervision is an integral part of Soviet sport and

plays a big part in the development of talent. The medical supervision of all people regularly engaged in physical activities is carried out by special sports medicine clinics, which are maintained by local sports committees and work in close co-operation with public health organizations. Some of the trade union sports societies have their own medical departments, and all national league squads in the major sports have permanent medical staffs. Official statistics show that there are over 300 sports medicine clinics and over 6000 departments of sports medical supervision and sports therapy in the country. All institutes of physical culture and as many as eighty medical colleges train specialists for these clinics and departments, which are regulated by the USSR Federation of Sports Medicine. In 1974 3900 doctors were employed in the clinics – roughly half a per cent of all Soviet doctors.

Every Soviet athlete must have a medical card and a personal case history which is registered at his local sports clinic or club. He is required by law to undergo examination at the clinic at regular intervals. In addition, he must secure a doctor's permission before taking part in major competitions. In certain combat sports such as boxing and wrestling the sportsman must be medically examined at the sports clinic before every contest; if he is competing in another town, he has to take his clearance certificate with him as proof of good health. It is the duty and responsibility of the physical education instructor, coach or team official to ensure that all members of the group are under constant medical supervision and that every athlete has the requisite permission to compete and train.

All Soviet representative teams have their own specialist physicians, who must keep in close touch with the staff of the local clinics which retain the athletes' medical history. Besides medical supervision, the job of these physicians is to give expert advice on the athletes' functional potential, capacity for work and optimum level of exertion. The key to sports attainment would seem to be the maintenance of a constant balance between the demands of a rigorous training programme designed to exploit fully each sportsman's functional potential and concern for his health and safety.

*Schools for Talent*

Young people who wish to pursue a sport seriously and to develop their talent may do so in one of several types of school (see Fig. 3).

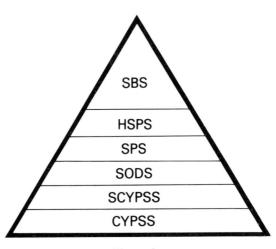

*Figure 3*
*Schools for talent*

SBS      = sports boarding school
HSPS     = higher sports proficiency school
SPS      = sports proficiency school
SODS     = sport-oriented day school
SCYPSS   = specialist children's and young people's sports school
CYPSS    = children's and young people's sports school

SPECIALIST DAY SCHOOLS

At the base of the pyramid is the children's and young people's sports school (CYPSS), which young people can attend outside their normal secondary school hours (they are, in fact, 'clubs' in the Western sense). There were over 5000 such schools with a membership of 1.75 million children in 1979. An attempt is made to spread the net as widely as possible, both to catch all potential talent and to distribute facilities fairly evenly between the republics. The Republic of Belorussia, for instance, is divided into six regions, each of which has approximately thirty-five such schools with an average of fifty coaches per school. Each school caters for an average of six sports. For example, the Republic School of Olympic Reserves in Minsk has some 800 children in six sections: water polo, handball, tennis, gymnastics, volleyball and chess (the chess section having six separate groups under three coaches).

Children are normally considered for a CYPSS on the recommendation of their school physical education teacher or at the request of their parents. Attendance and coaching are free. Although most of the schools take children at 11 years of age, for some sports they may accept them earlier or later. For example, entrants to swimming sections may be taken in at 7 or 8 (or earlier), while cyclists and speed skaters are usually admitted at 13 or 14. On the other hand, the Moscow Dinamo CYPSS has recently (1977) started up a gymnastics section for children between 4 and 6, who attend three times a week, and the Minsk Dinamo 'soccer nursery' takes young boys at 6 and 7.

How frequently the children train depends on the sport and the school, but coaching is usually intensive and classes are often long and frequent. In the First of May District of Moscow, for example, the CYPSS had, in 1978, preparatory groups of children between 11 and 13, who attended three times a week for two-hour sessions in the

*World chess champion Anatoly Karpov. Chess has a long tradition
and ample official support in USSR*

evenings; each group had fifteen members. Some of the top
groups did even more training: those working for their
Master of Sport ranking attended four or five times a week
for two-hour sessions. The USSR Sports Committee
devised a typical CYPSS training programme for all in a
statute on the schools published in 1970. The programmes
for swimming and figure skating shown in Tables 1 and 2
give some idea of how seriously the training is taken.

As is evident from Table 1, a 12-year-old swimmer
attending a school and working towards a third or second

*Table 1*

*Typical training programme for swimming in a CYPSS*

| Name of group | No. of groups | Age | No. of pupils in each group | No. of sessions per week | Length of each session (hours) |
|---|---|---|---|---|---|
| Preparatory | 6 | 7–8 | 12 | 3 | 2 |
| 2nd junior and 3rd adult ranking | 6 | 8–10 | 10 | 4 | 2 |
| 3rd and 2nd adult ranking | 4 | 10–15 | 8 | 4 | 3 |
| 1st ranking, Candidate Master of Sport and Master of Sport | 2 | 15–18 | 4 | 5 | 3 |

adult ranking will be in a group of about eight swimmers, attending three-hour training sessions four times a week. All swimmers at the school are expected to pass from novice to Master of Sport in between seven and eight years.

For figure skaters sessions are longer and more frequent than for swimmers. A 12-year-old figure skater working towards a first ranking would be in a group of five skaters, attending training sessions five times a week for four hours each session. As with swimmers, novices are expected to reach Master of Sport level by the time they leave the school. The load, in addition to school work, is by any standards considerable. It must be borne in mind, however, that Soviet children have a shorter school day (five hours, 8 a.m. to 1 p.m., in a six-day week) than do some Western children.

Originally it was intended that each CYPSS should culti-

*Table 2*
*Typical training programme for figure skating in a CYPSS*

| Name of group | No. of groups | Age | No. of pupils in each group | No. of sessions per week | Length of each session (hours) |
|---|---|---|---|---|---|
| 3rd junior ranking | 3 | 8–9 | 12 | 3 | 2 |
| 2nd junior ranking | 3 | 9–10 | 10 | 3 | 3 |
| 1st junior ranking | 2 | 10–11 | 8 | 4 | 3 |
| 3rd and 2nd adult ranking | 2 | 11–12 | 6 | 4 | 4 |
| 1st adult ranking | 1 | 12–13 | 5 | 5 | 4 |
| Candidate Master of Sport and Master of Sport | 1 | 13–18 | 6 or 4* | 5 | 4 |

* 6 for pairs, 4 for individual

vate up to ten sports, but today most concentrate on no more than three, some on only a single sport. The single-sport schools are known as specialist children's and young people's sports schools (SCYPSS). For example, each leading soccer club runs its own soccer SCYPSS, which provide a full course of training for talented young boys.

The aim of the CYPSS and SCYPSS is to make the best use of the limited facilities available in the USSR to give special coaching to young people in a particular sport so that they may become proficient, gain a ranking and graduate to a republican, city or Soviet national team. They are one of the vital keys to Soviet sporting success, especially in the Olympics. In fact, of the thirty-five sports pursued in the schools in 1976, only six were outside the Olympic programme: acrobatics, chess, modern gymnastics, handball, tennis and table tennis. The sports most practised were field and track events, basketball, gymnastics, volleyball, swimming and skiing.

The schools are therefore provided with the best resources: of the country's 60,000 full-time coaches and instructors in 1978, over half were working in the sports schools. It is certainly the case that the best coaches are drafted into the schools, and it is the prescribed duty of the country's best athletes to undertake regular coaching and to give displays in the schools. Another advantage of the schools is that they have access to amenities, particularly for technical sports, that are generally in short supply. In 1977, for example, over 80 per cent of the country's figure skaters and high divers, many of the swimmers and a third of all young gymnasts pursued their sports by the grace of these schools.

How much coaches and instructors are paid depends on the school. Some schools pay according to the number of children registered in each section, others according to results. Thus, a coach in the Leningrad District of Moscow may be earning 150 rubles a month (just over the average industrial earnings) by being paid by results, while one in the First of May District may receive only 100 rubles a month – although both coaches may have the same number of registered children. Some schools pay according to the number of hours worked by the coach. In the case of figure skating, however, the acrobatics coach, choreographer and pianist all receive a rate of pay which is calculated according to the number of hours they spend on a training session. The payments system is not free of abuses. It has been reported in the Soviet press that an acrobatics coach in Chirchik, Uzbekistan, obtained an extra 2536 rubles in one year for claiming for more hours than he had actually worked; when his time schedule was checked, it was discovered that he was claiming to have put in over twenty-four hours of training each day! Another coach at the same school had claimed for 'dead souls' – children who had not registered for his group.

The organizations responsible for financing and administering the schools are the local education authorities, the trade union sports societies and the big sports clubs run by Dinamo and the armed forces. Of the existing 5000 CYPSSs the education authorities are responsible for just over half, the trade union societies for a third and Dinamo and the armed forces for the remainder.

It is possible, from the age of 7, to attend a full-time 'sport-oriented' school, which combines a normal school curriculum with sports training (on the model of the 'foreign language'-oriented schools). These schools are not considered to run counter to the comprehensive principle, since they take in children from the neighbouring catchment area and provide them with extra instruction in sport and facilities that are superior to those available at 'normal' secondary schools. It should be noted that Soviet schools allocate no more than two periods a week to physical education, with no extra time for either games afternoons or swimming periods.

Above these schools in specialist training come the sports proficiency schools and the higher sports proficiency schools, which provide both extra-curricular training for schoolchildren and students and short-term vacation courses. The distinction between them is normally one of age: students between 16 and 18 attend the former, those 18 and over the latter.

In 1967 a new sports society for young people, *Yunost* ('Youth') was set up to co-ordinate the activities of all these schools and to ensure that minimum standards were established in regard to facilities, coaches, age and other entrance qualifications.

SPORTS BOARDING SCHOOLS

At the apex of the pyramid are the sports boarding schools, of which there were twenty-six in 1979. The USSR opened its first boarding school on an experimental basis in Tashkent in Central Asia in 1962; this was modelled on similar schools that had been established in the German Democratic Republic in 1949 (the year of that state's foundation). The first Soviet schools were soon followed by others – at first one in each of the fifteen republics, then some in certain provincial centres. It was not until 1970, however, that a special government resolution set an official seal of approval on their existence. Before that they were given virtually no publicity. By 1970 about twenty were in existance and another twenty-four were said to be scheduled for the immediate future; all the same, their rate of development seems to have slowed down somewhat in the late 1970s. In 1979 there were twenty six sports boarding schools. While some concentrate on a single sport, others cultivate a range, though usually no more than four (the Leningrad Sports Boarding School, founded in 1972, trains children in ten sports, but this is exceptional). Significantly, only sports in the Olympic programme are taken up by the sports boarding schools.

They follow other special boarding schools (those designed to cultivate mathematical, musical and other artistic talents, for instance) in adhering to the standard Soviet curriculum for ordinary schools, but their timetables allow for an additional study load in sports theory and practice. Their aim is to permit pupils to obtain the school-leaving certificate in addition to acquiring proficiency in a particular sport. Boarders are accepted from between 7 and 12 years old, depending on their sport, and they stay on until 18 – a year longer than at normal schools.

It would seem axiomatic that such schools should possess first-class amenities. The one I visited in 1970 in

Tallinn, Estonia, had four sections: gymnastics, basketball, volleyball, field and track events. It had three gyms, a 25-metre indoor swimming pool, a ski centre, a stadium, and courts and fields for a variety of team sports. In Uzbekistan the Tashkent school takes pupils in soccer, swimming, field and track events and gymnastics. The school grounds cover an area of 20 hectares and include a three-hall wing for gymnastics, indoor and outdoor swimming pools and an indoor running track.

Not all such schools are as well equipped. Children at the First of May School in Moscow have to travel to other parts of the city to use a swimming pool and an indoor running track. The Leningrad school which I visited in 1975 and again in 1978 had no facilities at all to speak of, except a small swimming bath and residential accommodation for 270 boarders; plans had, in fact, been approved for an indoor stadium, a swimming pool, a medical research centre and new residential wings.

Boys and girls are normally invited to attend the boarding schools on the basis of their performance in republican school games. With the consent of their parents, they can enter the school if they pass a rigorous ten-day entrance examination and medical tests. The allocation of periods to sport in the timetable rises with each successive year of the course. For example, at the Tashkent school 11-year-olds studied their chosen sports for six hours a week, 12- and 13-year-olds for eight hours, 14- and 15-year-olds for ten hours, 16- and 17-year-olds for twelve hours, and 18-year-olds for fourteen hours a week. Despite these tough schedules, it is asserted that the pupils have a better than average health and academic record: the physical and intellectual aspects of the training they receive apparently supplement and reinforce one another. A gymnastics boarding school in Dnepropetrovsk claims better academic results (as well as better discipline and health) than ordinary local schools; and in 1978 the head of the Leningrad school,

Leonid Shapiro, insisted that his principal concern was academic work: 'General education first, sport second' was the school motto.

The Tallinn school had a teaching staff of fifty and seventeen qualified coaches to instruct the 750 pupils in 1970. The syllabus included such specialist subjects as the psychology, the history of physical education and educational philosophy. Virtually all the pupils were boarders, although some returned home at the weekend; fares home for holidays and weekends were paid by the school. Annual expenditure amounted in 1970 to 650,000 rubles (that is 850 rubles per pupil), most of which was provided by the Estonian Ministry of Education and the remainder by the USSR Ministry of Education. This sum covered the provision of hostel accommodation, instruction, sports equipment and clothing (all supplied gratis to boarders) and an especially nutritious diet (the daily food expenditure per pupil – eighty four kopecks – was virtually double that of ordinary boarding schools).

The Leningrad school had 570 pupils in 1978 (65 per cent boys, 35 per cent girls), twenty-seven academic staff and sixty-three part-time coaches. In addition to the finance it received from the city education authority and the central ministry, it obtained some assistance from twenty Leningrad industrial enterprises, which acted as 'patrons' of the school – a fairly common system in the USSR. The headmaster explained that the school was very popular: for each of the ten sports in the school some 300 children were selected out of 1000 applicants; 150 were taken to special summer camps and after a further test, thirty were accepted as boarders. Inevitably, some children were subsequently rejected during the first four years of the school's existence, but this practice was now said to be declining: 120 out of 480 pupils left in the first year, eighty in the second and forty in the third. By 1978 the drop-out rate was said to be down to under twenty.

An advertisement in the daily sports paper *Sovetsky sport* for the Znamensky Brothers Sports Boarding School, which opened in Moscow in 1973, attracted over 900 letters from 823 towns and villages all over the country during six weeks of 1973. The school has winter and summer stadiums, seven Merited Coaches of the USSR and the Russian Federation and twelve Masters of Sport on its staff. Some 150 children were selected from among the initial applicants for tests, and fourteen days were taken up with medical examinations. Several candidates were rejected on academic grounds; others were accepted on the condition that their school marks improved. As with other schools, a minimum sports requirement for entry to forms six to ten is a third adult ranking in the chosen sport – a considerable achievement for children between 13 and 17. In the case of the Znamensky school an exception was made for children with unusual physical attributes such as above-average height: 13-year-old girls over 1.7 metres tall were accepted 13-year-old boys over 1.8 metres tall.

The motive for the establishment of these sports boarding schools has been the conviction that talent in sport has to be developed from an early age. It is regarded as natural and advantageous to bring together children with an instinctive aptitude for sport in the 'controlled' environment of a residential school, where they are provided with the best coaches and amenities, nurtured on a special diet, supervised constantly by doctors and sports instructors and stimulated by mutual interest and enthusiasm. Moreover, early specialization, especially in such sports as running, swimming and gymnastics, is regarded as essential to the attainment of high standards and success in present-day international competition. In the opinion of the above-mentioned Leningrad headmaster, 'Sports boarding schools are the only way to win world championships in today's competitive sport.' It is no secret that their ultimate aim is to produce Olympic winners. It is also

*Young gymnasts at a sports school in Minsk. Talent in sport is treated as equivalent to talent in music and art*

openly acknowledged that the Soviet leadership regards success in the Olympics as an indicator of a nation's health and power, as conferring considerable prestige on winning nations. As many as 70 per cent of the USSR's Olympic medals have been gained in field and track events, swimming and gymnastics. In the first three of these the USA and East Germany have an overall superiority which, it is thought in the USSR, they have attained both by providing excellent facilities for young athletes and swimmers and by carefully selecting and coaching these youngsters at schools and colleges.

The Soviet sports boarding schools are not without their

critics within the Soviet Union. Some contend that they lack depth and cannot produce a sustained flow of world-class athletes: they compare sporting prodigies with early-flowering plants, which make a colourful showing, as it were, in early spring, only to fade when 'normal' flowers are blooming. An article in the monthly magazine *Fizkul'tura i sport* (*Physical Culture and Sport*) claims that no more than five soccer players made the grade from an original group of 1500 in specialist sports schools; research results published in the monthly *Teoriya i praktika fizicheskoi kul'tury* (*Theory and Practice of Physical Culture*) in 1976 showed that the drop-out rate among first-year students in all sports schools in the country is in the order of 80 per cent. Other detractors decry the privilege implicit in the existence of the schools and the possible encouragement of an asocial lifestyle conductive to 'starsickness'. The much respected economic 'reformer' Professor Birman, in a letter to *Sovetsky sport* (*Soviet Sport*) in 1974, recalled Lenin's words: 'Libraries should take pride in the number of readers they attract, not in the rare books they keep in their repositories'; surely, Professor Birman asked, 'Lenin's words apply equally to sport?'

Some educationalists fear that the range of experience offered to pupils in the schools is restricted by the demands made by sport on time and energy, and they are concerned that academic work is being overshadowed. There is also the problem of the time and effort involved in getting from classroom to running track. The biggest stumbling-block so far, however, seems to have been the opposition of some parents who are anxious about the slackening of family bonds or eager for young Ivan or Olga to 'get on' and uncertain about the status of sport as a career. One source has admitted that

the sports boarding schools do not show the slightest popularity among parents, for a number of reasons. First, parents do not like the word *internat* ['boarding school' – perhaps because of its association with the institutionalized care of the deprived]. Their logic is simple: 'Can't I feed my child myself?' Then the word 'sport' puts them off; they find it embarrassing to tell their neighbours, 'My Sasha is in a *sports* school.'[1]

This was written in 1971, when the boarding schools were in their infancy; there is some indication that they are now more readily accepted by parents.

All the same, the nature of such comments and the apparent effectiveness of parental opposition suggest a relatively low status for sport as a vocation, at least in the opinion of a fairly important section of the Soviet public. Perhaps such teething troubles are inevitable. Despite the quite frank criticisms and the debate on sports schools in the Soviet press, the schools seem to have passed the test, and the future of serious Soviet sport would appear to lie with them. Whatever the prospects, the concept of the sports boarding school has far-reaching implications for theory and practice. The purists may well argue, with some justification, that this is yet another step in the race for medals and irrational glory that should find no place in a socialist state. The pragmatists, on the other hand, may consider it a natural and sensible development in a centrally planned state to concentrate resources to maximum effect in order to win victories in today's highly competitive and specialized world of sport.

## NOTE

[1] *Moskovskaya pravda*, 26 February, 1971, p. 4.

# Chapter 5

# *Professional Training*

As one would expect in a country where most fields of endeavour are administered centrally, the Soviet Union has a well-co-ordinated system of professional training for every level of the sports movement. The personnel may be engaged as full-time or part-time staff (the latter including referees, instructors, voluntary officials, and so on, who devote part of their spare time to sport). Among the full-time sports personnel there are those directly employed in sport and physical education (coaches, physical education teachers and recreation officers at workplaces and sports specialists) and those responsible for administration and the construction of sports amenities. In the first part of this chapter we look at one of the full-time categories of personnel, coaches, and a part-time group, referees; the second part deals with professional training within education, research and publications.

*The Contribution of Professional and Voluntary Personnel*

**COACHES**

Coaches are the most authoritative figures in Soviet sport. Not only are most coaches skilled specialists in their own sport, with a detailed knowledge of a scientific discipline and medicine, but they are also responsible for the moral conduct of their charges. And when their pupils win high honours, the coaches share in them.

They receive specialist training (see below) in a variety of courses: in 1977 three-fifths of all professional coaches had completed no less than a four-year full-time course in higher education (or a five-year evening or correspondence course), while the remainder possessed diplomas from other types of courses. Without such qualifications it is impossible to obtain employment in coaching on a full-time basis. And since it is officially prescribed that every sports centre and every sizeable factory should employ its full complement of coaches, and since every sports school has to have a coach in each sport it practises, the range of employment is extensive. How well the USSR is served by coaches may be judged by the claim that in no Olympic sport is the ratio of coaches to top-ranking athletes less than 1:12; in most it is less than 1:7. In some sports (gymnastics, show jumping, speed skating, athletics, swimming, diving, modern pentathlon and figure skating) it is 1:3 or less. It is noteworthy that these sports are the ones in which the USSR has been making a big effort to excel internationally.

For the country's leading coaches status and material rewards can be high. They may aspire to the title Merited Coach of the USSR, introduced in 1956 for coaches responsible for training Masters of Sport, champions and record-breakers at Soviet, European, world and Olympic tournaments, or for introducing new training and instruction methods. Top coaches may also gain the title of Merited Coach of a particular republic for outstanding success with republican sportsmen, which is equivalent to the highest awards and titles in literature and the arts. Since 1967 coaches have also been able to qualify for gold medals and bonuses for training sportsmen who win international honours; the first beneficiaries were the two long-serving coaches of the Soviet ice hockey team, Chernyshev and Tarasov. A number of coaches have also featured in the USSR 'honours list': after the 1976 Montreal Olympics, as mentioned above, three coaches were among the eight people honoured with the Order of Lenin. It is clear that the Soviet coach is officially highly esteemed and is rewarded accordingly. The penalty for failure, on the other hand, as elsewhere in the world, is normally the sack – as successive coaches to the USSR soccer team have discovered.

Professional coaches are engaged on a full-time basis and receive a more or less fixed salary; it is a statutory rule that the normal working time of coaches and recreation officers at all workplaces should not exceed forty-one hours per week. How much a coach earns depends on his qualifications, length of service, honorary titles and success rates of his charges and on the geographical location in which he is working (the Siberian rate of pay is double that of the European areas of the country – as is the case with other occupations). A senior coach at a children's and young people's sports school with a full ten-year school education and a dozen years' coaching experience would receive some 115 rubles a month. A senior coach with a higher sports qualification, with the title of Merited Coach of the USSR and ten years' coaching experience, who is engaged at a ten-day training camp (preparing his charges for competition) would receive a monthly salary of 170 rubles (120 basic plus 20 for his title plus 30 rubles extra for work at the training camp). Since many coaches work overtime, they receive additional increments: thus a senior coach with higher education, ten years' coaching experience and a Merited Coach title would receive 210 rubles a month if he worked 150 hours instead of the set 100 hours. The top Soviet coaches would appear to be earning between 300 and 400 rubles a month (just over double and treble the average industrial earnings respectively).

Coaches may also be employed on a part-time basis, in

which case they are paid according to the amount of time they spend with their pupils; these part-timers make up nearly two-thirds of the total professional coaching personnel. In 1974 just over three-quarters of them were fully qualified – that is, they had diplomas or degrees. Apart from these professional coaches, there are many coaches who work on a voluntary, unpaid basis at factories, farms, offices and sports societies. They may be concerned with coaching in a particular sport, with instruction in general sports and games or with physical exercises at places of work and study. Although no payment is officially made for this type of work, a great variety of token badges, certificates and banners may be won, up to the honorary title Outstanding Worker in Physical Culture. Part-time instructors are encouraged to obtain some coaching qualifications and are given time off from work, with pay to attend three-week intensive courses. Further, all graduates of sports schools are automatically qualified to work as part-time sports instructors.

In 1978 there were nearly eight million such part-time coaches and instructors – an average of one part-timer to every twelve sports participants in the country as a whole.

## REFEREES AND SPORTS OFFICIALS

Since the present supply of trained personnel cannot keep pace with the rapidly growing sports movement at all levels, a great deal of responsibility is given to the people who undertake such work on a voluntary basis. There are currently some four million referees, all part-timers, who are given time off from their workplace (on full pay) for attending training courses and for officiating. Referees are ranked by experience and qualifications as All-Union, republican, first, second or third category; the remainder simply bear the title 'referee' (by individual sport). Every sports club is supposed to have its own core of referees who are responsible for conducting tournaments and arranging the training of new referees. Over a quarter of all referees bore the top title, All-Union Referee, in 1970, which is some indication of how concerned the Soviet authorities are that all sports officials should be well trained.

Another two million part-time officials are engaged in the activities of sports clubs and societies, as recreation officers, administrators and members of the various councils and audit commissions of the sports committees. Neither they nor the referees are paid for their work.

*The Training of Physical Education Teachers*

Soviet secondary and higher educational establishments teach a large number of students who become physical education teachers, coaches and officials in schools, colleges, sports societies, clubs, factories and farms. The range of physical education teaching and research institutions is shown in Table 3.

*Table 3*
*Professional training institutions (1977)*

| Type of training establishment | Number |
| --- | --- |
| Institutes of physical culture | 25 |
| Physical education faculties at universities and colleges | 90 |
| Specialist physical education schools | 26 |
| Physical education departments at colleges of education specialising in physical education | 73 |
| Schools for coaches | 20 |
| Physical culture research institutes | 4 |

Authority over the institutes of physical culture is shared by the central Sports Committee and fifteen republican committees on the one hand, and the republican education ministries on the other. The two oldest and most famous institutes are the Lesgaft Institute of Physical Culture in Leningrad and the State Central Order of Lenin Institute of Physical Culture in Moscow; the other twenty-three are spread among the republics and major provincial centres.

Students for the physical culture institutes are normally accepted for one of two degree courses: education or sport.

EDUCATION DEGREE COURSE

On graduation after a four-year course, students become physical education teachers with the right to work in schools and colleges, sports societies or urban and rural sports groups. The curriculum includes four disciplines which all students must take, plus a special course of seminars and an optional course.

(a) *Compulsory subjects*

   (i) Social sciences, comprising history of the Communist Party of the Soviet Union, philosophy, political economy, scientific communism and scientific atheism.

   (ii) Education, comprising psychology and sports psychology, educational theory and history of education, history of physical culture, sports management, theory and methods of physical education, a foreign language and civil defence.

   (iii) Medicine and Biology, comprising human anatomy and physiology, biochemistry, hygiene, sports medicine, treatment of sports injuries and massage.

   (iv) Sport, comprising athletics, gymnastics, team sports and outdoor recreation, skiing, swimming, speed skating, weightlifting (men only) and additional sports. This course covers the theory, methods and technique of teaching these sports. Some 1130 hours, or 36 per cent, of all teaching hours are allotted to the basic sports listed under (iv) and another 280 hours to additional sports.

(b) *Special seminars and optional course*

(i) Students may choose from a variety of seminar courses, all of which are designed to enhance knowledge of research methods used in sport. the courses include statistics, applied mathematics, cybernetics and electronics.

(ii) In the second year a student may take options either in the history of physical culture or in educational theory; a third-year student may take either theory and methods of physical culture or physiology; and a fourth-year student must choose as a speciality either a particular sport, 'production gymnastics' (physical exercise at workplaces) or therapeutic gymnastics.

During the course the student is also obliged to spend thirty weeks in practice – both educational practice at a school and organizational practice in a factory or farm recreation group. The student normally completes his practice as a recreation officer at a children's youth (Young Pioneer) camp during the summer vacation.

In addition to the subjects mentioned above, there are several general, non-examinable courses (such as aesthetics, ballroom and folk Dancing, elocution, Soviet literature and a number of sports) which the student may choose to attend voluntarily. Moreover, all students must retake their fourth-stage GTO test, obtain a second-class ranking in two (optional) sports and the title of Referee Second Category in two sports.

Undergraduates who have passed all their term tests and sessionals, fulfilled all their practical tasks and completed the four-year course are admitted to state finals in the following three subjects: human physiology, theory and methods of physical education and scientific communism.

This course is more or less uniform in all physical culture institutes, with the exception of those in Moscow and Leningrad, which accept only first-ranking sportsmen-students and offer a more intensive course (see Appendix 2); their students also receive higher grants. These are the two most prestigious physical culture institutes in the country.

SPORTS DEGREE COURSE

For this degree course the student specializes in a particular sport and receives the qualification of Coach–Instructor, with the right to work in any sports organization, from a local farm group or factory sports club to a city, regional, republican or national sports society team.

The course is basically the same as the education degree course. The social sciences curriculum remains the same, the only difference being the inclusion of coaching. In the medicine and biology section the student studies biomechanics and sports technology as separate subjects, and medical supervision and sports injuries replace sports medicine. The sports section is dominated by the student's chosen sport (750 hours), but in addition he had to study athletics, gymnastics, team sports, swimming, skiing and weightlifting (men only; women take modern gymnastics), and their teaching methods (590 hours in all).

It may be appropriate at this point to compare this course with professional training elsewhere. In the opinion of two British lecturers in physical education,

The essential requirement of a 1st Ranking in the specialist sport for entry of students to the physical culture institutes assures a basic practical level and experience for future coaches which, when coupled with the time given to that activity in professional training (750 hours), guarantee a high-level practitioner. Our experience of College of Education courses in the United Kingdom indicates a time allocation to the specialist activity (if one is permitted) in the order of 40 hours and it is hardly surprising that technically we are falling behind.[1]

It may be added that to be aware of the comparative standing of one's own system of professional training, one has to be able to study foreign systems. All Soviet students at physical culture institutes must study a foreign language (and the foreign sports system) in the first two years (210 hours per annum); after that it is optional. By contrast, no physical education course in Britain has provision for foreign-language study as a compulsory component of the course. It is hardly surprising, therefore, that the vast majority of physical education students and teachers in Britain know no foreign language and are, of course, unable to study foreign systems and teaching materials at first hand.

The time devoted to educational practice for students at Soviet institutes of physical culture on the sports degree course is the same as that for the education course, teaching practice being spent in a secondary school, sports school, sports society or club, while organizational practice takes place in a youth camp or sports group.

The special seminar course is identical to that included in the education course, but the optional coursework is monopolized by the student's chosen sport. Where facilities allow, a student may undertake research into his sport instead of completing some of the normal coursework. Stage 4 of the GTO programme has to be retaken and, in addition, the student must gain a first ranking in his chosen sport, at least a third ranking in two other sports and a first-category referee's certificate in his chosen specialism. Final examinations consist of general and sports physiology, the theory and teaching of the specialism, and scientific communism. If a student has written an adequate dissertation on his chosen sport, he is excused examination in his special subject.

As Soviet young men are eligible for national military service over a period of two and a half years, it is incumbent upon all male students to undergo some military training during their time at the institute; indeed, most institutes have their own departments of military training. Female students are obliged to take a course lasting 360 hours in medicine and remedial gymnastics in lieu of conscription.

The physical education faculties at colleges and universities come under the jurisdiction of the USSR Ministry of Secondary and Higher Education and the corresponding republican education ministries. Graduates as a rule become teachers of physical education at secondary schools. The course lasts four years and closely follows that of the education course at institutes of physical culture, as do the final examinations. Subjects excluded are statistics, wrestling, weightlifting, an additional sport and methods of teaching it and introduction to a specialism. Teaching practice is normally spent partly in a secondary school, partly in a youth camp (three weeks, during the third year) and partly in charge of an outdoor activities course (two weeks).

The specialist physical education schools (*tekhnikums*) come under both the republican sports committees and the education ministries. They train physical education teachers for schools and coaches in individual sports mainly for rural areas. Most of the entrants are accepted at the age of 16 straight from general secondary school; they undergo a course of between two years (for those who leave school at 17 and over) and three years (for those who leave school at 16). The course is broader and less intensive than that followed in higher education: subjects include human anatomy, physiology, hygiene, psychology, education, the theory and practice of physical education, the history and organization of sport, sports management, gymnastics, athletics, team sports, skiing, speed skating, swimming, outdoor recreation and a sports specialism. Final examinations include subjects similar to those specified for institutes, with the exception of the social science subjects. The reason for their exclusion may be that graduates are expected to take up jobs requiring less political awareness and involving less responsibility than those offered to institute graduates. Finals, therefore, comprise physiology, the theory and practice of physical education and the chosen sport.

Students must do teaching practice in schools, rural sports clubs and youth camps; they must also meet the following standards in the sports programme and rankings: GTO Stage 4, the equivalent or near-equivalent of the second sports ranking, a third ranking in one sport featured in the curriculum and the third-category referee ranking.

The departments at colleges of education specializing in physical education fulfil more or less the same function as the specialist physical education schools mentioned above in training teachers for schools. The study course is three years, entrants being taken at the age of 16, after eight years of general education. The only difference is that the departments include biology in their course. Their immediate authority is the republican ministry of education and the republican sports committee. With the drive to overcome the shortage of physical education teachers in the countryside, they have recently introduced one-year courses for mature students who will return to teach physical education in rural areas, and six-month courses for people wishing to do sports work in the countryside.

Schools for coaches are usually attached either to an institute of physical culture or to a specialist physical education school. Although they do take students at the age of about 16 straight from school, they are chiefly concerned with evening and correspondence courses for experienced sportsmen who wish to gain a coaching certificate during their sports career. Courses last between two and three years for internal students, plus a year extra for external students. All entrants for the full-time courses are obliged to take an entrance examination in Russian, chemistry and physics, to hold not less than a second sports ranking and to have at least eight years of schooling. The course, which is neither as long nor as academic as that offered to coaches at the institutes of physical culture, consists of general subjects (history, geography, literature, foreign languages and so on), education, medicine, biology and sports subjects. In addition, a further 105 hours are scheduled for refereeing, photography and proficiency in the chosen sport. Since part of the entrance requirement is that students must hold a high sports ranking, no additional demands are made during the course as regards sports practice and rankings. Finals consist of examinations in physiology, social studies and the chosen sport.

In 1976 the school for coaches at Moscow's Central Institute of Physical Culture became the country's Higher Coaching School, in order to provide 'republican and club teams with well qualified coaches in a whole range of sports'. It accepts only coaches and former athletes who have a higher education, extensive experience either as coaches or as athletes in national and republican teams and who have demonstrated teaching skills. The course lasts two years. As one example, the soccer coaches section of the school was launched in 1976 with thirty-five students (including past internationals Fedotov, Kaplichny, Malofeyev, Asatiani and Khmelnitsky). Its aim was said to be to train 'skilled coaches of junior teams and league clubs by means of a two-year course that includes contemporary coaching methods, foreign languages and the disciplines necessary to the modern soccer coach'. The course was scheduled to include guest lectures by leading world authorities on soccer: Helmut Schoen of West Germany,

Milanic of Yugoslavia, Michels of Holland, Gurski of Poland and others. The decision to call on lecturers from abroad is certainly a radical departure for Soviet teaching generally, and it reflects a concern to improve the performance of Soviet soccer teams internationally.

It should be pointed out that most physical education qualifications, like higher degrees generally, are obtained through correspondence and evening courses and are designed to help people to improve their qualifications (students are granted time off with pay). In the case of part-timers, the courses normally take an extra year to complete. In addition, in-service training is widely available for all sports officials, referees and part-time instructors. Refresher courses are *compulsory* for all professional coaches and teachers of physical education; as a rule these consist of two- to three-month courses during the summer vacation (in the case of schoolteachers).

At the end of their courses, for a period of three years, graduates are assigned to a job and a region in accordance with their qualifications and, where possible, their preferences. However, this can result in a placement unwelcome to the student, in an outlying rural area or provincial centre in Central Asia or Siberia. From the state's point of view, this is the best way of distributing expertise evenly over the whole of the vast country, especially in the more backward rural areas, and of enabling the student to repay his educational debt to the community (all education courses being free in the USSR). It is my impression that a good many students accept this placement system in good part and that they are aware of their debt to society and willing to serve the community. However, assessments differ; a fair-minded colleague of mine has told me that he is of the opinion that

each graduate tries to line up the best job for himself that he can prior to graduation. The state thereafter simply rubber-stamps

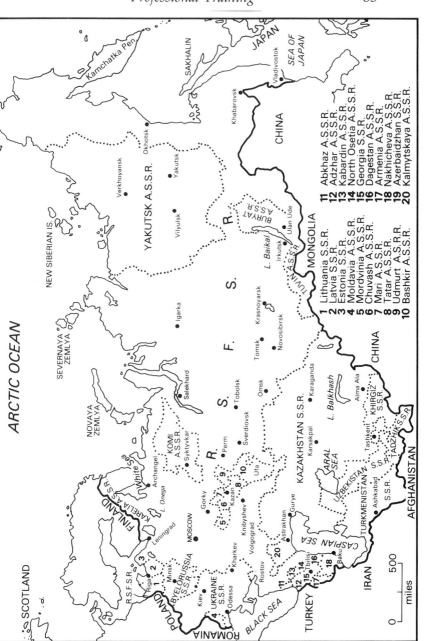

Figure 4  *The Union of Soviet Socialist Republics, which extends over half of Europe and a third of Asia*

his appointment as 'approved'. The graduates who finally end up by getting posted to Hicksville are only a small, residual minority, comprising in general those students who have relatively poor grades and have therefore not succeeded in gaining a post after their own wishes.

Whatever the actual situation, the placement system does, of course, guarantee students employment upon graduation.

One last point of relevance here is that *all* Soviet students do physical education and sport as a compulsory part of their course for the first two years at college or university. They must have a record of full attendance and must pass their preliminary examinations in the subject before being permitted to continue into the third year of their normally five-year degree course.

*Research*

Research into physical education and sport is an integral part of the Soviet sports movement. It is conducted at a large number of higher educational establishments (including all the institutes of physical culture and the physical education faculties), at medical colleges, polytechnics, at the USSR Academy of Medical Sciences (most important of all, at one of the latter's institutes, the Research Institute of Physiology and Physical Education) and at two separate physical culture research institutes in Moscow and Leningrad. Five institutes of physical culture – in Moscow, Leningrad, Tbilisi, Kiev and Minsk – run special three-year courses for researchers (four-year for part-time students). A documentation centre for books, periodicals and films concerned exclusively with sport and physical education is located in Minsk. Altogether, the Soviet Union is said to have some 4000 people working on research in the area of sport (1979).

Students who wish to register for postgraduate studies in sport or physical education are required to pass entrance examinations in Marxist–Leninist philosophy, a foreign language and their specialism. Once accepted, they cannot spend more than three years as full-time students; during this period they have to pass a number of exams known as the Candidate Minimum (including a foreign language) and prepare a dissertation which has to be defended publicly. Only when they have also shown evidence of new scientific and practical knowledge, of their ability to conduct independent research and of their profound theoretical knowledge of the chosen field of study can they receive the Candidate of Sciences degree. A postgraduate is also required to deliver lectures to students and to conduct classes in his specialism. A certain number of specialists with publications and practical experience behind them are permitted to register as part-time researchers; they are given more time to pass their Candidate Minimum examinations and to defend their dissertation.

All academic degrees awarded by institutes of higher learning must be approved by the Higher Certification Commission. It has the right to revoke degrees if they have no specific application or value for science and production.

Unlike many Western universities and colleges, Soviet institutions do not present a *carte blanche* to their postgraduate students in selecting themes for research. Nor do the institutions themselves have complete freedom of choice. Research is an integrated effort, in which a department, college, region or republic receives an assignment from a higher body such as the government, a trade union, the education or health ministry or the USSR Sports Committee; all the institutions involved may then pool their efforts to work on the assignment. In several institutions all junior researchers may participate in a single major assignment under the guidance of a senior researcher or professor. In 1975, for example, the USSR Sports Committee and the Committee on Science and Technology jointly approved a five-year sports research plan for 1976–80. The programme involved all the institutes of physical culture and embraced the following areas: organization of physical education, sports training, sports history, professional training, sports equipment and amenities, and overall planning.

As is evident, efforts are made to stress the applied nature of sports research and to maintain close coordination between scholars and scientists on the one hand and sportsmen and coaches on the other. Moreover, a scientific and technological study of sport and its related sciences is obviously regarded as vital to a real understanding of the significance of sport in everyday life and work and as the basis for improved performance. In the early 1970s research into the sociology of sport was also being undertaken – an area hitherto largely unexplored in the USSR. Much attention is also paid to the medical side of sport: medical departments exist at all physical culture institutes and colleges, and future coaches and teachers have to attend courses on the prevention and treatment of athletics injuries.

The extent of research into the technical aspects of sport testifies to the careful preparation that goes into sports performance and the seriousness with which the authorities regard the role of sport in society. It provides an insight into the official concern with what are believed to be the major functions of sport: to help improve productivity, to maintain a physically fit nation ready for military action, to advertise the communist system through international sports success and to contribute to a fuller life for all citizens.

As in other research spheres, bonuses and gold medals are awarded for outstanding work: in 1977 the USSR Sports Committee made ten such awards for three types of research: work on the theoretical and sociological problems of physical culture; research into training and teaching; and medical and biological work on physical education and coaching.

## Publications

As the function of the mass media is largely to promote education rather than entertainment, their role in Soviet society and therefore in sport – is particularly important. Sport is, after all, a valuable (indeed, necessary) component of everyday life – and it is the task of the mass media to popularize sport and the benefits that are supposed to accrue from it. Moreover, sport and sporting publications, by virtue of their popular nature, are regarded as convenient vehicles for political information. All this gives Soviet sports periodicals and books a rather serious air by Western standards. On the other hand, they are completely free of obsession with 'stars', gossip, sensation and big-money sports (horse racing, for example) that dominates many Western publications.

In 1979 there were forty-six sports periodicals with a circulation of over eight million. Of these, fourteen were published centrally in Moscow for the whole country and the rest were published for local populations, often in a non-Russian language. In daily circulation among national newspapers, sports journals come seventh, *Sovetsky sport* (*Soviet Sport*) standing above the teachers' and servicemen's professional newspapers. The single most popular sport in terms of the number of periodicals devoted to it (four) and of circulation is chess. Nearly all the major sports have their own magazines, which generally come out once or twice a year. The major sports periodicals are listed below.

*Sovetsky sport*, the organ of the USSR Sports Committee, has been published since 1924. It is a popular four-page newspaper costing only two kopecks and is published daily except Mondays. It contains information about the performance of teams and athletes at home and abroad, political news and any resolutions on sport, criticisms, readers' letters and the results of sudden spot checks on sports organizations in any part of the country. (In 1977 it published as many as 207 articles and letters critical of organizations and personnel involved in sport, including exposés of 'fixed' soccer matches; many of the complaints were investigated and improvements made.) The paper has a daily circulation of four million copies, is printed in thirty-five Soviet cities and has three supplements which are sold separately: the two weeklies, *Futbol* (*Football*) – which changes to *Khokkei* (*Ice Hockey*) in winter – and *Chess 64*, and *Sport za rubezhom* (*Sport Abroad*), which appears twice a month. *Sovetsky sport* and its supplements have some 50,000 foreign subscribers.

*Fizkul'tura i sport* (*Physical Culture and Sport*), founded in 1922, is a popular, well illustrated monthly and also an organ of the Sports Committee. It costs thirty kopecks, contains between forty and fifty pages and had a monthly printing of over 400,000 copies in 1976.

*Teoriya i praktika fizicheskoi kul'tury* (*Theory and Practice of Physical Culture*) is a theoretical and technical monthly journal, also published by the Sports Committee. It costs forty kopecks, averages eighty pages and had a monthly circulation of some 19,000 in 1976. As its name implies, it is a serious journal containing about-thirty articles an issue and much interesting material and research data of value to coaches, sportsmen, physical educationalists and sociologists. It consists conventionally of the following sections: general introductory articles, often political or historical; training, techniques and tactics; physiology, sports medicine; sport and young people; sport in everyday life (sociological problems); physical education in college; detailed technical surveys in the form of replies to readers' questions; sport abroad; reviews; reports on conferences.

*Sport v SSSR* (*Sport in the USSR*) is a monthly illustrated magazine, first issued in 1963 and mainly printed for foreign consumption as a supplement to the general glossy magazine *Sovetsky soyuz* (*Soviet Union*). It is published in Russian, English, German, French, Spanish and Hungarian, averages thirty pages and costs thirty kopecks.

*Fizicheskaya kul'tura v shkole* (*Physical Culture in School*) is a monthly illustrated journal published by the USSR Ministry of Education since 1930 and intended mainly for physical education teachers. It costs thirty kopecks, averages fifty pages and had an average circulation of 120,000 copies in 1976.

A very informative sports magazine, which includes English, German, French and Spanish translations, is the glossy thirty-five-page *SKDA Sportivnoye obozrenie* (*Sports Review of the Sports Committee of Friendly Armies*), published four times a year since 1972 and printed in Berlin by the German Democratic Republic Military Publishers. It gives information on sport and the military in the communist world (with the notable exception of China and Albania), and is published in each of the (Soviet-aligned) communist states.

The Soviet sports administration has its own publishing house in Moscow, *Fizkul'tura i sport* (*Physical Culture and Sport*), which is reputedly the biggest in the world. In 1977 it accounted for half the total production of Soviet sports literature: 182 publications – books, manuals, albums and brochures – with a total output of nearly ten million copies. Even this large number is said to meet only half the demand.

To sum up, just how much the Soviet sports movement owes its attainments to a trained and co-ordinated leadership should be evident from this chapter. The USSR could not have achieved its success in the world of sport without its highly trained coaching and administrative leadership.

Not everyone in the West would wish the professional training in their own country to be as standardized and as centrally controlled as it is (formally at least) in the Soviet Union. However, there is much in the Soviet system that is worthy of consideration. Among the aspects of the system that merit attention are the following:

1. The integral study of science and medicine for sports personnel;
2. The guaranteed and rational employment of all physical education graduates;
3. The encouragement given to men and women of mature years, especially ex-athletes, to obtain qualifications in sport and physical education through correspondence and evening courses;
4. The obligatory study of a foreign language and foreign sports systems;
5. The national policy that draws all the agencies together and gives experienced coaches such an effective influence over development;
6. The precise job definition and formal pre-service and in-service training given to coaches, and the after-service outlets for channelling their expertise;
7. The system of sports rankings that gives athletes and coaches targets to aim for and that provides officials with guides for selection;
8. The free centres of excellence open to pupils with talent and staffed by top coaches and sports medics;
9. The high status of sports medicine and its integration with the sports movement.

## NOTE

[1] M. A. Speak, V. H. Ambler, *Physical Education, Recreation and Sport in the USSR* (Lancaster, 1976), p. 86.

Chapter 6

# *Gymnastics*

Gymnastics is the foundation of physical culture in the USSR and has long enjoyed widespread popularity. From early in the morning onwards – exercises are broadcast daily before breakfast – Soviet people of all ages and from all walks of life come into contact with one or more forms of gymnastics every day. This intensive exposure to the sport in its various forms helps to explain the general appreciation of gymnastics in Soviet society and the admiration and respect accorded to gymnasts.

The concept of gymnastics is interpreted more broadly in the USSR than in the West and covers a number of different activities: modern rhythmic gymnastics ('artistic gymnastics' in Russian); body-building ('athletic gymnastics' – which has had an uncertain existence, given official disapproval of the dandified culture of the body and the excesses associated with the sport in pre-revolutionary Russia and the West); work-break exercises ('production gymnastics', which many employees engage in at their workplace, much as Western workers take a tea or coffee break); remedial gymnastics, which are frequently prescribed to employees following an industrial injury; and school gymnastics, which constitute 70 per cent of the school physical education programme. The term, of course, also covers 'sporting gymnastics', known simply as gymnastics in most English-speaking countries, and this is the activity to which this chapter is devoted.

*Therapeutic gymnastics at a sanatorium. Regular exercise is regarded as important at all ages*

## The Development of Soviet Gymnastics

Sporting gymnastics goes back to the earliest days of organized sport in tsarist Russia. A Swede, de Pauli, opened the first Gymnastics Institute in the Russian capital, St Petersburg, back in 1830. The sport was officially recommended to the nobility as extremely beneficial for health and education. It was also useful for military training – the original prime function of the sport. Just as the German *Turnvereine* of Jahn, the Czech Sokol movement of Tyrs and the Scandinavian gymnastics movements of Ling and Nachtegall in the nineteenth century were attempts to regenerate nations after military disasters, so Russian gymnastics was intended to refurbish the Russian aristocracy, especially after the Crimean War.

The first gymnastics club came into being in St

Petersburg in 1863; it was followed in the same year by the renowned Palma Gymnastics Society and, in 1868, by the Moscow Gymnastics Society. Pyotr Lesgaft, the 'father' of Russian physical education, introduced gymnastics on the Prussian model in to the Russian imperial army in 1874. Shortly afterwards he established gymnastics courses for army officers and, in 1896, for civilians. The first national federation for any sport, the Russian Gymnastic Federation, was set up in 1883 on the initiative of a group of social reformers which included the writer Anton Chekhov. He expressed the hope, cherished by many sports enthusiasts, that the Federation's members 'would be the people of the future. The time will come when everyone will be as fit and strong; there lie the nation's hopes and happiness.'

As elsewhere in Europe, gymnastics became the basis of physical education in schools, although schooling was confined to a narrow section of the population. With its small base among the aristocracy and encouragement from the rising industrialists, gymnastics had become popular enough at the turn of the century for a Russian team to be sent to the Olympics of 1912 and actually to win medals.

The Russian Revolution of 1917 brought the hopes of Chekhov nearer fruition. In the immediate post-revolutionary period gymnastics was the foundation of the sports campaign. Besides requiring little equipment, it was a suitable medium for social policies such as the campaigns for fitness and hygiene, the social liberation of women and military preparedness. It was believed, too, to satisfy that desire for an aesthetically pleasing life which was worthy of the liberated man and woman of the first workers' state. Mass gymnastics displays of the 1920s became extremely popular and often took the place of competitive sports events (which, as mentioned above, were frowned upon on ideological grounds): some 18,000 people, for example, took part in a vast gymnastics display at the new Red

Stadium to mark the opening of the Second Congress of the Third International in 1920. Anatole Lunacharsky, the first education minister, even invited Isadora Duncan to Soviet Russia in 1921 and helped her set up her own academy in Moscow (she actually took Soviet citizenship, married the poet Yesenin and undoubtedly had a considerable influence on the development of 'artistic gymnastics', although she only stayed two years in Moscow).

Gymnastics, nevertheless, had its opponents – largely because of its association with foreign systems, its nationalist overtones (from the old Pan-Slav Sokol movement) and its lack of 'teamwork'. During the 1920s gymnastics was actually banned from some tournaments and even excluded from the schools. All the same, this was a temporary aberration and the First Gymnastics Championships, held in 1928, attracted a large entry; in fact, more people participated in gymnastics than in any other sport at this time.

With the onset of the 'industrial revolution' at the end of the 1920s, opponents of gymnastics were swept aside and, following a government resolution of 1933, gymnastics became the basis of the sports movement and of physical education in schools. Linked as it was with ballet and other forms of cultural expression, gymnastics was used, too, as a means of drawing athletes into the orbit of culture. The aesthetics of human movement were thought to represent artistic expression at its best; a new and dynamic cultural force, it was believed, would emerge through the graphic symbolism of gymnastics, calisthenics, the dance and mass formation displays, as through the newly founded *spartakiads*.

Although no Soviet gymnasts took part in bourgeois international contests prior to the war, Soviet gymnasts did compete in the Workers' Olympics held in Antwerp in 1937 and they won the team championship. It is asserted that by 1941 Soviet gymnasts had attained the top world standards in technique. After the war circumstances and policies changed radically, and the Soviet Gymnastics Association became affiliated with the Fédération Internationale de Gymnastique in 1948. Soviet gymnasts made their international debut at the 1952 Olympic Games, winning nine gold and eleven silver medals, and both the team and individual titles for men (Chukarin) and women (Gorokhovskaya) – a success that was repeated in 1956. Since then, however, the Soviet men's team has been placed second to that of Japan, though Soviet women have won every Olympic title.

The galaxy of outstanding gymnasts who altered the entire complexion of the sport during the 1950s included such athletes as Galina Shamrai, Sofia Muratova, Polina Astakhova and Larissa Latynina among the women, and Victor Chukarin, Boris Shakhlin, Grant Shaginyan and Yuri Titov among the men. Since then Soviet gymnasts have not monopolized the sport to quite the same extent; Japanese men and Romanian, Hungarian, East German and American women have come to the fore. Nonetheless, many brilliant gymnasts, particularly among the young women, have graced the sport – Larissa Petrik and Natalia Kuchinskaya in the 1960s, and Ludmilla Turishcheva, Olga Korbut, Elvira Saadi and Nelli Kim in the 1970s.

*Gymnastics Today*

The popularity of gymnastics in the USSR today may be judged by the fact that 750,000 people are said to engage in it regularly. Of these, three-quarters have gained a sports ranking and as many as 600 have reached Master of Sport level. To train these gymnasts the country has 20,000 gymnastics coaches and an extensive network of clubs and schools.

The age at which one should take up gymnastics is a

debatable issue among Soviet specialists; it has had to be reconsidered of late in view of the marked reduction in the age of top gymnasts. It has been pointed out that the average age of all five winners in the women's section (beam, floor, vault, assymetrical bars and overall) has fallen in the four Olympics between 1964 and 1976 from 22.8 to 16.6 years. The respective reduction for men (in seven events) was 26.3 to 25.4 years. What is more, while men have remained more or less stable in height and weight over the four Olympics, the average height and weight of women gold medalists has fallen from *1.62 metres and 54.6 kilograms in 1964 to 1.53 metres and 46.2 kilograms in 1976.*

While members of the USSR gymnastics squad in 1971 took up the sport seriously at 12.7 years of age on average, by 1977 the average starting age had fallen to 9.8. In a recent poll it was revealed that three-quarters of all Soviet gymnastics coaches recommend that boys should begin gymnastics at the age of 10–11, girls at 8–9, although they mostly agree that the first two or three years should be devoted to building up all-round fitness. Some individual coaches, however, are introducing youngsters to the sport seriously at an even earlier age. In 1978 the Moscow Dinamo Club, for example, started training a group of children between 4 and 6, who attend sessions in the gymnasium three times a week for an hour and a half on each occasion. The first Soviet coach to train nursery-age children was the controversial Innokenty Mametiev who, largely by virtue of his own efforts, built up a very successful gymnastics club in the small Siberian town of Leninsk-Kuznetsky. In 1977 four of his girl gymnasts were ranked in the country's top twenty gymnasts (Filatova, Glebova, Serkova and Komarova). However, he is certainly not without his critics: a journalist in the popular daily newspaper *Komsomolskaya pravda*[1] accused him of 'crippling children spiritually' by his severe regime, of 'depriving children of their childhood', of being interested solely in their gymnastics results and of shutting his school doors to all but the talented.

## GYMNASTICS SCHOOLS AND PROFESSIONAL TRAINING

If a young person shows inclination and talent, he is likely to be accepted into a children's and young people's sports school or into one of the special gymnastics schools which children attend, free of charge, outside their normal school day. The high standard of Soviet gymnastics has been achieved almost entirely through the work done in these schools.

How seriously the sport is taken in these schools (or 'clubs', in the Western sense) may be gauged from the programme stipulated by the USSR Sports Committee (see Table 4).

Although conditions inevitably vary in practice, training regimes possess the following standard features:

*Table 4*
*Typical training programme of a gymnastics school*

| Name of group | No. of groups | Age boys | Age girls | No. of pupils in group | No. of sessions per week boys | No. of sessions per week girls | Length of each session (hours) boys | Length of each session (hours) girls |
|---|---|---|---|---|---|---|---|---|
| Preparatory | 3 | 9 | 8 | 15 | 2 | 2 | 2 | 2 |
| 'Young Gymnast' | 3 | 10 | 9 | 15 | 3 | 3 | 2 | 2 |
| 3rd ranking | 3 | 12 | 11 | 12 | 3 | 4 | 3 | 2 |
| 2nd ranking | 2 | 13 | 12 | 8 | 4 | 3 | 3 | 3 |
| 1st ranking | 2 | 15 | 13 | 6 | 4 | 4 | 4 | 3.5 |
| Candidate Master of Sport | 1 | 17 | 14 | 4 | 5 | 5 | 4 | 3.5 |
| Master of Sport | 1 | 18 | 15 | 3–4 | 5 | 5 | 4 | 3.5 |

1 Pre-entry selection based on mental and physical suitability.
2 Detailed attention to physical fitness and preparation, and regular compulsory medical check-ups.
3 Ballet lessons for every gymnast from beginners onwards, given by a choreographer who is normally expert at foot and transitional movements in floor exercises.
4 Absence of the teacher's 'helping hand' ('spotting') at all levels of learning (excellent physical fitness and the use of large pits filled with foam rubber and of progressions obviating the need for 'spotting').
5 Theoretical instruction in basic techniques, training, physiology, psychology and rules of competition.
6 Individual, written planning and recording on a daily basis, with a three-five year plan (each gymnast keeps a daily diary of his workout).
7 A ratio of two coaches per twenty-five or thirty beginners, increasing to one coach per three or four gymnasts in the Candidate and Master of Sport categories.

During a visit in the late summer of 1978 to the gymnastics school in the Belorussian capital of Minsk (officially named the Minsk Specialized Gymnastics Children's and Young People's School of Olympic Reserves), it was interesting to note that the school caters for boys and young men only between the ages of 6 and 26 for the four disciplines of gymnastics, acrobatics, trampolining and choreography. The choreography coach is, in fact, an ex-ballet dancer and People's Artist (a not unusual progression in Soviet gymnastics). All the full-time coaches at the school have a higher education. Each gymnast keeps his own personal diary in which he records all results, load, stress and daily mental and physical state of health.

The 7-year-olds attend the school four times a week, arriving for each two-hour daily session at 9 a.m. (they attend normal secondary school in the afternoons). The eleven-year olds attend six days a week for three-hour sessions. The annual cycle of training consists of preparatory work for the first three months of the year, followed by eight months of competitive gymnastics (ten internal and twenty-two external competitions) and one month of transitional work. The weekly timetable is as follows:

Monday – introductory work, comprising 400–500 distinctive exercise movements

Tuesday – heavy training day

Wednesday – heavy training day

Thursday – light training day

Friday – medium training day

Saturday – heavy training day, followed by a sauna

Sunday – day off.

Given this fairly rigorous schedule, it is perhaps hardly surprising that the drop-out rate is relatively high. Of the initial intake of 330 to the Minsk school, only 10 per cent survived to continue two years later.

While the initial testing is confined to height, weight, the parents' physical measurements and the children's gymnastics results, it later becomes more thorough as the children undergo extensive tests at the Minsk city sports clinic. The tests cover the heart, blood, urine and muscle tissue. Besides access to the more specialized clinic in the city, the school also has its own medical treatment centre on the premises.

Altogether the USSR has some 200 such special gymnastics schools, although only three of them are exclusively for boys.

If a budding gymnast shows exceptional ability, he or she may be accepted into one of the gymnastics boarding schools or a sports boarding school with a gymnastics section. In the school I visited near Tallinn, 12-years-olds spent twenty-five hours in a six-day week on standard subjects, and eight hours on gymnastics, two hours on swimming and two hours on general physical education. In the last form, at 18 (students stay a year longer than at normal schools so as to complete the standard educational course), they devoted twenty-three hours a week to sport, including nineteen hours of gymnastics. Roughly the same number of hours must be spent on academic work.

If a gymnast does reach the top of the sport, it is expected that he or she will continue study in higher education, however disjointed that study may become because of the demands of training and competition. A gymnast will enter further education at the level appropriate to his school qualifications and interests; if he chooses to prepare for a sporting career, he will probably enrol in a school for coaches or an institute of physical culture (see Chapter 5). At the latter a full-time course in gymnastics lasts four years and includes, besides the standard pedagogical subjects, coaching methods, competition organization, the maintenance of equipment, techniques for each piece of apparatus, tumbling and modern gymnastics. Each student must also acquire a judging certificate.

A high proportion of active gymnasts take correspondence courses in coaching and teaching during their competitive career. The courses normally last five years, although for top gymnasts the course may be extended to up to ten years if they are involved in extensive training, competition and travel. It is a strict rule that all correspondence-course students must be on campus for classes and tests six weeks out of every year.

Gaining a degree or diploma is seen as a preparation for a career after active gymnastics comes to an end. Of course, the fact that coaches are former performers is hardly remarkable and must be so everywhere in the world. What is noteworthy about Soviet sport generally is that it is regarded as perfectly natural for *all* sportsmen to prepare during their active sports career for a job, usually in coaching, when they retire from competition. Latynina, Muratova and Astakhova, for example, are all national coaches. Yuri Titov took over the Gymnastics Section of the USSR Sports Committee in 1969 and is currently President of the Fédération Internationale de Gymnastique. Grant Shaginyan runs a gymnastics club in his native Armenia. Ludmilla Turishcheva, who retired from competition in 1978, at the age of 25, after thirteen years in competitive gymnastics, obtained her gymnastics coaching diploma from the Moscow Institute of Physical Culture during her active career and is now working on her doctoral dissertation at the Rostov Institute of Education (her theme is 'the emotional effects of pre-performance tension among female gymnasts on their actual performance'). Concurrently, she is training a group of children between 11 and 13 at the Rostov Sports School. Olga Korbut spent seven years studying history at the Grodno College of Education, only graduating when she finally retired from active gymnastics in 1978.

Being a gymnastics champion brings its rewards. Olga Korbut, for example, has had her own two-roomed apartment next door to her coach's family in her home town of Grodno. She has been able to travel widely and to enjoy high esteem in the Soviet Union (though by no means the adulation she received in the West; the 'star treatment' meted out by the mass media in the West has virtually no place in the USSR). With the privileges goes the obligation to give displays and lectures regularly and to undertake forms of public service. Larissa Latynina, for example, was a city councillor in Kiev for several years. Ludmilla Turishcheva, formerly team captain and Komsomol secretary for the USSR women's gymnastics team, was a candidate for membership of the Communist Party in 1977. During her career she also often gave displays at factories and clubs, occasionally travelling far afield to construction sites and oilfields in Siberia. She has frequently said that she regards this public service as an important responsibility for all athletes. It would, however, be naive to imagine

*Olga Korbut, who has probably attracted more people to sport than
any other athlete in history*

that all Soviet champions are as public-spirited; it is a matter for the individual conscience of each athlete. Some respond; some do not. Nevertheless, many do seem to regard it as an important source of inspiration and a means of keeping them in touch with common people.

## The 'Secrets' of Soviet Gymnastics Success

Soviet gymnastics success is attributable to a variety of factors, some general and some specifically Soviet. Of prime importance is efficient organization embracing both central planning and the extensive groundwork which is laid at the start of the career of both gymnast and coach. Emphasis is also laid upon a consistent, co-ordinated, long-term programme for the training of gymnasts. Table 5 shows a typical chart, published in 1978 by the eminent gymnastics specialist V. M. Smolevsky. It is, of course, an 'ideal' chart and not every Soviet gymnast has a career that accords exactly with these requirements. It also makes no mention of the sports boarding schools which now play an increasingly important role in educating promising young gymnasts. However, the chart is interesting in that it gives a clear indication of the consistent training schedule that supports the entire career of every Soviet gymnast.

Efficient organization also consists in a meticulous study of training methods. The bulk of the sixty-page, twice yearly journal *Gimnastika* (*Gymnastics*), the monthly *Teoriya i praktika fizicheskoi kul'tury* (*Theory and Practice of Physical Culture*) and scores of gymnastics manuals are all devoted to detailed research into the mechanics of movement (of turns, twists, landings, vaults, somersaults and so on), psychological preparation and foreign experience. Although by comparison with Western specialist journals on gymnastics, the contents of *Gimnastika* would not be remarkable, its circulation certainly would: some 35,000 copies for each issue in 1977.

*Table 5*

*Typical long-term preparation chart for top-class gymnasts*

| Stage | Selection and initial training | Start of special training | Extended special training | Attainment of proficiency | Attainment of peak results | Post-peak |
|---|---|---|---|---|---|---|
| Age   Boys | Up to 9 | Up to 12 | Up to 15 | Up to 18 | 18 and over | |
|      Girls | Up to 8 | Up to 10 | Up to 13 | Up to 16 | 16 and over | |
| Programme | General developmental exercises | Basic exercises and the rankings programme | Basic combinations and the rankings programme | Special requirements; model combinations; Fédération Internationale de Gymnastique programme | | Rankings programme |
| Standards | Basic standards | Junior rankings | 2nd ranking up to Candidate Master of Sport | Candidate Master of Sport to Master of Sport | Master of Sport to Master of Sport International Class | Rankings standards |
| Institutions | Nurseries and primary schools | Children's and young people's sports schools (CYPSS) | CYPSS | Specialist CYPSS | Higher sports proficiency school and national squads | Sports societies and physical education institutes |

The USSR also benefits from highly qualified coaches and good facilities at top levels, a co-ordinated calendar for each gymnast – that is, an annual training–competition–rest schedule – a far-flung network of training and retraining, preparation for a future career in coaching, a standard rankings system and extensive state support for gymnastics.

In a discussion I had in 1978 with the ex-gymnast and current FIG President Yuri Titov, he explained the Soviet gymnastics competition calendar. In the late August national championships 100 boys and 100 girls compete, out of whom nineteen of each sex are chosen (by results in the championship) and ranked accordingly. This 'seeded' list is then checked at the end of September in the School Gymnastics Championships (up to the age of 18). Then the final squad is selected and invited to a three-week training session prior to the World Championships. The daily training schedule that is recommended to all aspiring gymnasts is as follows: 6 a.m. rise; forty mins special exercises; four hours intensive training every day except Sunday.

As gymnastics is an intellectual sport, in Yuri Titov's opinion, it is important for every gymnast to take an active interest in reading, theatre, ballet and music, to obtain a higher education and to become a highly trained specialist.

The efficiency and resources of the system would count for little, however, without personal motivation. And it is here that Soviet gymnasts, like their counterparts in Eastern Europe and Japan, score highly: in their attitude to training, their hard work and their dedication to gymnastics – and, not least of all, in personal qualities such as self-discipline, confidence and creativity. They possess, too, an artistic quality of performance, particularly evident among the women in the free exercises, that is uplifting and represents a fusion between sport and art. This balletic grace and musical expression is undoubtedly associated with the Russian cultural heritage. But the sheer force of example of the Soviet gymnasts has produced very successful imitators and rivals, notably in Romania, Czechoslovakia and East Germany. A parallel Soviet influence can be seen to be at work in figure skating and ice dancing.

In combination, all these factors constitute a compelling reason why Soviet gymnasts have done so well in world competition. Yet their contribution to sport goes beyond winning medals. Before the 1972 Olympics, at which Olga Korbut, Ludmilla Turishcheva and Elvira Saadi performed with such grace and skill, there were some 500,000 participants in gymnastics in Britain. Today there are over three million practising weekly. A similar boom has occurred all over the Western world – due almost entirely to the young Soviet gymnasts. For some, no doubt, the novelty drained away with the first beads of perspiration in a cold gymnasium, but many have remained in the sport – attracted initially by gymnasts like Olga Korbut, but detained by the thrill of contest, the warmth of companionship and the satisfaction of striving for fitness, grace and artistry.

It is to the credit of Soviet gymnastics that the sport has become so popular among participants and spectators alike all over the world.

## NOTE

[1] 14 January 1976, p. 4.

# Chapter 7

# *Soccer*

Soviet soccer merits a chapter to itself for a number of reasons. Unlike gymnastics, it is not a sport at which the USSR has excelled internationally; it therefore cannot be described as an elite sport to which prime attention has been given for prestige purposes. It will also be profitable to analyse why Soviet soccer has not done particularly well in the major world tournaments.

It is a sport, too, which has its roots firmly in the foreign clubs of pre-revolutionary Russia. That is not to say that the institution of soccer has not been shaped also by processes generated by Soviet attempts to build a new society. There are, indeed, several fundamental distinctions that have to be drawn between *futbol* and football, as we shall see.

The most salient reason for highlighting Soviet soccer is that it is the most important spectator sport in the USSR in terms of both match attendance and TV audiences. As it is a game on which millions of spectators pin their hopes and fears, their loyalties and prejudices, this fact also has certain implications for fans and players alike – and for the authorities. It will be interesting to observe how Soviet society deals with fan mania (or even whether it exists at all), how players cope with the pressures that a premium on winning exerts upon them and how the soccer administrators deal with bonuses, 'stars', rough play and other problems attendant upon modern professional soccer. There is the additional question of commercial income from

the sport and how this is allocated among competing interests.

As we shall see, the problems that stem from encouraging a mass spectator sport and the public's identification
with it have accompanied Russian soccer ever since it was
introduced (mainly by Scots and Englishmen) at the end of
the last century. They are worthy of attention here because
they appear to parallel some of the problems facing soccer
in the West, and because they provide evidence of notable
deficiencies within the Soviet sports system. Without an
assessment of these problems, a full picture of Soviet sport
would be incomplete.

*The Origins of Russian Soccer*

The first football game introduced in Russia was rugby, the
bold initiator being a Scot, a Mr Hopper employed in a
Moscow cotton mill. But rugby was outlawed in 1886 by the
authorities, who considered it brutal and liable to incite
riots. Soccer, however, fared better. It, too, was introduced
by foreign residents in Russia, who played among themselves initially and then in mixed teams, including some
Russian students, cadets and clerks. Mostly the British and
the Germans played among themselves; the first refined
game emerged, as in Britain and the USA, from the British
schools and colleges which attempted to codify the laws.
The united English college students' team played under the
name Gloria, and English and German employees in St
Petersburg formed the Victoria Football Club. The team
played matches against the Scottish Circle of Amateur
Footballers, Germaniya Football Club, the English Football
Club and a team from the British diplomatic corps which
bore the impressive title of the Superior Society of the
British Colony which then, as now, played soccer, tennis
and cricket – but *not* against the Russians.

The first recorded soccer match among Russians was played in the interval between cycling races at the Semyonov Hippodrome in St Petersburg in 1892. This 'kick-and-rush' game was followed in 1896 by the first Russian match to be played according to the rules adopted by the English Football Association. The first Russian league was started in 1900 in the capital and was made up exclusively of foreign residents' clubs, with a membership mainly of Scots, English and Germans.

But as Russian soccer attracted more players and spectators, friction grew between the previously dominant foreign teams and the newer Russian clubs. One cause was the monopoly of the soccer administration by foreign residents, who were accused of showing bias against Russian teams and players. It was not long before Russian teams formed their own league and boycotted the foreign teams. An immediate cause of the disaffection was said to have been an incident in a fixture between the Russian team Sport and the English Nevsky. The English referee, V. S. Martin, had sent off a Russian player, Chirtsov, after a tackle on an English player, Sharples. A Russian sports paper of the time takes up the story:

The League Committee's decision is to disqualify Chirstov for a year and to let off Sharples with a 'caution'! This year we have Sharples the Throttler! Next we shall have Jim the Stabber and Jack the Ripper! Match reports will soon read like crime records. Will that gladden the hearts of Russian sportsmen? Certainly not. The British, in their typical high-handed manner, with their big voting majority, are banning a Russian who is totally blameless and letting off a man who is obviously dangerous but is one of their own! Let Russian clubs band together and form their own league.[1]

And so it was, thus marking the end of foreign influence on Russian football.

The Russian Football Association was created in 1912, a

dozen years after the German and nearly fifty years after the English Association. It immediately became affiliated with FIFA. In the same year the first Russian city soccer championships took place, with five cities competing (St Petersburg, Moscow, Kiev, Odessa, Kharkov). It is noteworthy that the Russian Football Association had forbidden any city team competing in the championships to include more than three British players. All the same, Odessa, which won the 1913 city championships, played four British men – and was promptly reprimanded.

By the outbreak of World War 1, Russian soccer was so widespread that as many as nineteen clubs with ninety-seven teams were competing in the St Petersburg League, twenty-five teams made up the Moscow League and several other cities had their own leagues. In 1912 the Russian Football Association sent the first team of Russian nationals abroad to represent their country in the Olympic Games, held in Stockholm. The team, wearing yellow shirts with the tsarist two-headed eagle emblem on the chests, lost to Finland and, disastrously, to Germany (0–16) – a defeat that dented Russian national pride. That was the first and last time a Russian national team was to compete abroad in tsarist times.

It is significant that Russian working men were largely excluded from organized soccer. Until 1914 no registered team or league could admit them; the amateur snobbery of Britain, as perceived by the Russians, was applied to the letter in Russia, and all artisans and manual labourers were barred from participation. Consequently, they tended to organize independently of the middle class and state institutions – as they were to do politically in the 'Soviets' (workers' councils) – in factory *druzhiny* (fraternities) and *dikie* ('outlaw') groups. These played on rough and open ground, watched by their fellow workers, and sometimes even served as a cover for guerrilla training. Most workers were therefore not integrated into the system through the medium of games, and the workers' unregistered sports clubs developed political overtones as a result of their semi-clandestine nature. The British diplomat Robert Bruce Lockhart, who was in Russia during World War I, wrote that had British entrepreneurs been able to spread the passion for playing soccer more quickly in Russia, the Whites might have won on the playing fields of Moscow what they lost in the Reading Room of the British Museum. He regarded the introduction of soccer by the British industrialists and employees then resident in Russia as 'an immense step forward in the social life of the Russian worker and, if it had been adopted rapidly for all mills, history might have been changed'.[2] Perhaps Mr Lockhart overplays the political power of soccer and underplays that of Marx and Lenin, but he does focus attention on the use of sport, especially soccer, by some regimes to divert the populace from political action and to encourage conformity.

The Soviet authorities were, then, to inherit from tsarist Russia a soccer system that was already fairly well developed in all the major urban centres of the Empire.

*The Spread of Soccer*

After the 1917 Revolution, despite the confusion and far-reaching 'paper' resolutions, the tsarist soccer competitions, leagues and clubs persisted largely unmolested by the new regime. (A total of fourteen teams contested the Eleventh Spring Cup in the Russian capital in 1918, all of them having been formed prior to the Revolution.) It was not until the mid-1920s that the newly formed Supreme Council of Physical Culture took over or disbanded the former 'bourgeois' clubs. In fact, most of the old clubs were simply appropriated lock, stock and barrel, with their premises, teams and colours, and given new names: Unitas became Pishchevkus (Food Co-operative), Kolomyaki became the Lenin Stadium Club, Putilov Works became the Red Putilov Works and so on. The clubs were now run by trade unions, which increasingly came in for criticism from the Party and the Young Communist League for encouraging professionalism. One journal issued a broadside: 'In a number of trade union football clubs, all attention is being concentrated on a tiny group of players to the detriment of the great mass of young people.'[3] Signs of professionalism were already apparent in the Leningrad League: in 1925 a disqualification committee was set up to 'prevent dirty play' and player transfers were banned. In the following year the first Soviet footballer popularity poll was held.

Despite the problems associated with it and despite being outlawed by some organizations because of its association with professionalism and the evils of its bourgeois past, soccer retained its popularity throughout the 1920s as the country's national sport. by 1928 the number of registered players was 250,000, much higher than the pre-revolutionary figure. What is more, the government encouraged the game in town and country as a means of attracting people to sport and good health, of arousing their identification with a local club or town and inculcating a team spirit that was felt to be part of the new ideology. Exhibition matches were played in small towns and villages, even in the far-flung corners of the old empire where soccer had never been seen before. Soccer and other organized sports were used, for example, to help break the hold over local populations of religions, especially all-embracing faiths like Islam, that impinged upon large areas of social life – including sporting activities which, religious leaders considered, interfered with work and distracted men and women from serious spiritual concerns. Any enticement of Central Asian youth, particularly young women, into the sports activities organized by the Soviet authorities was regarded as a breach of the feudal bey and the religious order, as encouragement for the 'progressive' values supposedly imparted by sport, which undermined those aspects of religion spurned by the central authorities as 'irrational', 'superstitious', 'mystical' and 'subservient'. The propagation of soccer sometimes backfired, however, and the sport was used as anti-Russian propaganda by local religious leaders. In one Central Asian village the Russian soccer teams were driven out by an enraged public after the mullahs had said that the Russians had brought them 'the head of the devil' (the ball) which 'jumped and rained blows on them, bringing them misfortune'! It is perhaps natural that the primitive origins of the game should have been recalled by pre-industrial people unaccustomed to games that were highly controlled and circumscribed by rules which ensured that the excitement of the struggle did not carry the players too far.

During the 1920s soccer was the only sport in which matches took place between Soviet and other national teams, mainly Scandinavian and Turkish. Contacts might have been more extensive but for the refusal of certain governments (the Austrian, the Spanish, the Czechoslovak) to grant entry visas to Soviet players. The first 'international' match in Soviet times is said to be that played during the Second Congress of the Third International in 1920. The team consisted of foreign delegates at the Congress; it was captained by a young Scottish Temperance Society delegate, William Gallagher (later to become president of the British Communist Party), and included as goalkeeper the writer and ex-Harvard footballer John Reed (author of *Ten Days that Shook the World*). Understandably, the foreigners lost by a heavy margin to a representative Moscow team.

*Leagues, Cups and Stars of the 1930s*

As we have seen, the 1930s witnessed the great campaign

to turn the USSR from a backward agrarian into an advanced industrial nation. It was a period in which virtually every aspect of life was devoted to the success of the plan. Sport was no exception.

One concomitant of this drive was the encouragement of competitive spectator sports like soccer. Sport became, in effect, professionalized, and players were induced to treat their performance as part of their contribution to the fulfilment of the plan. Excellence in sport was the equivalent of the achievements of the shock-worker in industry. This had two purposes: at home the proficient player was to inspire emulation among the mass of casual sportsmen and to engender pride among spectators. The international significance of sport stemmed partly from the implications of Stalin's doctrine of the possibility of building socialism in one country, a doctrine that revived in a new form the whole cult of Russian messianism. Although it was to be a couple of decades before Soviet players and teams in any large numbers actually ventured into international competition with 'bourgeois' sportsmen, skilled performers capable of world-class performance were to be encouraged and given every inducement to perfect their skills.

Soccer was an ideal agency for these policies. In 1935 nationwide soccer leagues and cup competitions were started; previously, championships in soccer had been contested by city teams. Henceforth, sports societies like Spartak, Dinamo and Lokomotiv had full-time teams in every major city that competed in one of the four national divisions; each division contained initially seven or eight teams until 1938, when Division 1 was enlarged to twenty-six teams. The next year it was reduced to fourteen, the level at which it has roughly remained to this day. A total of 296 teams contested the Third USSR Cup in 1938.

The 'professionalization' of soccer was not without its problems or critics; the pressures of winning resulted occasionally in attempts to win at all costs. For example, during a Division 1 'derby' match in Leningrad between Leningrad Dinamo and Moscow Dinamo on 24 July 1937, three home-team players were taken to hospital and the fans rioted. Ever since, every major soccer match in the USSR has been patrolled by a 'wall' of soldiers and police who ring the ground between fans and the pitch.

Acknowledgement of the importance of soccer and its top players came with a government decision in 1937 to award the country's supreme honour, the Order of Lenin, to the Dinamo and Spartak sports societies. Just a couple of months earlier the rankings system had been introduced and the Merited Master of Sport title conferred on twenty-two sportsmen, including ten footballers. Further evidence of the official concern for soccer came in 1936, when twenty-one of the fifty sportsmen and sports officials who received medals and orders were footballers. This was the first time that individual sportsmen had featured in the 'honours list', which is some indication of the attention and adulation that heroes in sport, especially soccer, were receiving in the 'cult' period. Subsequently, the well-known footballers Lev Yashin, Igor Netto and Valentin Ivanov were to receive the Order of Lenin – the Soviet equivalent, perhaps, of Stanley Matthews's knighthood in Britain.

Throughout the 1930s soccer continued to be the most popular male sport in summer. Women also took up the game and there were enough female teams to form a women's league in 1940, although they did not survive the war. The number of soccer teams and players increased rapidly: in 1939, as many as 2000 teams entered the national Cup Competition, and the following year a record total of 2150 teams entered the qualifying Cup rounds. Internationally, sports contacts grew and Soviet teams played Bulgarian, Czech, Basque, Swiss and Turkish teams. The 1930s were the years *par excellence* for mass spectator sport and displays; they were becoming increasingly popular as a

*Bronze statue of soccer players by Joseph Chalkov, Tretiakov Art Gallery, Moscow. Sport and artistic expression are often linked*

means of advertising sport and encouraging emulation and civic pride, and as a 'safety valve' for the pressures built up in the austere working and living conditions of this period rapid industrialization. (As just one example of such displays, a green fibre carpet was rolled across part of Moscow's Red Square in 1936 and a soccer match was played on it between two Moscow Spartak teams.)

Attempts were made to popularize other organized team sports. Rugby (Union), for example, was introduced into several Soviet schools and colleges in 1926 and again in 1932. It was not until 1934, however, that two teams were assembled in Moscow for exhibition matches. In October 1935 the first inter-city rugby tournament took place between Moscow and Minsk (the former winning 6–0). Two years later a national championship was contested by two Moscow teams and teams from Minsk and from Gorky. Facilities nonetheless were rather primitive and the game did not stimulate sufficient popular support to warrant the government's continuing with its efforts to implant it in the Soviet Union. It was not until the late 1950s that Soviet rugby teams once more began to be formed.

The decision taken in the mid-1930s to stratify in sport, to distinguish a more or less professional group of sportsmen from the main body, was fully in keeping with the country's social development and its accompanying official values: in industry and agriculture, reward and prestige went to the workers and teams that attained the best results. The ordinary people were to be inspired by the efforts of people with whom they could identify, persons whose faces they could see in the newspapers, on street hoardings and on factory and farm boards of honour. Even more than their counterparts in industry, the soccer 'stars' began to receive large sums of money and were given priority in respect of apartments and scarce commodities for winning championships. Seen in its wider context, this was part of the general trend towards the creation of an elite when the cult of Stalin was at its height. All these practices were initiated in the mid-1930s and continue to this day.

## Post-War Developments

With the conclusion of the war and the ratification of a new national target – to catch up and overtake the most advanced capitalist powers (and that included in soccer, too) – the USSR was set to test its footballing skills against the best in the world. Spearheading the assault on the bourgeois fortress was the Moscow Dinamo soccer team which, only a couple of months after the war, accepted invitations to visit Sweden, Norway and Britain. It played four matches against leading British clubs without defeat (beating Cardiff 10–1 and Arsenal 4–3, and drawing with Chelsea 3–3 and Glasgow Rangers 2–2) – and this at a time when British soccer was still considered to be supreme in the world. The following year, 1946, for the first time two Soviet sports federations, those for soccer and weight-lifting, joined the respective international bodies.

Two irrational features of the immediate post-war upsurge in patriotism and xenophobia (after the terrible experience of Hitler's invasion) were the purge of famous pre-war sportsmen and the attempt to 'Russify' sports terminology.

Purges were not new to the sports movement; indeed, practically the whole sports administration had vanished in the purges of the latter part of the 1930s. But attacks on players for 'counter-revolutionary activities' were novel. The four footballing Starostyn brothers, Nikolai, Alexander, Andrei and Pyotr, for example, who were household names before the war, were arrested immediately afterwards and all received between eight and ten years in labour camps because, it is alleged, 'they had all been abroad and told friends about foreign life'.[4] Their time abroad, in fact, had been spent with Soviet soccer teams playing against foreign opposition. The second brother, Alexander, is reported to have told a fellow inmate of his at the labour camp in Kotlas in the Soviet Far North that the NKVD (security police) had been 'most interested in his sweaters, suits and hats bought abroad'.[5] Nearly thirty years later, when he published his autobiography, Andrei Starostyn was still only able to make a veiled reference to the 'missing' decade: 'People's destinies were varied and difficult in the war years. Life took its toll. But when I returned to Moscow in 1954 after several years *beyond the Arctic Circle* the capital was already constructing a new life.'[6] These arrests paralleled those of people tainted with foreign associations in other spheres, and they reflected the general Stalinist neurosis about 'infections' of all kinds from abroad. It may be, too, that the purges of well-known figures served warning on Soviet sportsmen about to compete with foreigners that they needed to be careful about nurturing personal contacts abroad and spreading tales at home about the foreign way of life.

The second aberration in post-war sport was the purge of sports terminology, most of which, of course, was English. This occurred in the context of the Great Russian chauvinism that prevailed at that time. In a speech to the Party Central Committee in 1946 the Party spokesman responsible for ideological and cultural affairs, Andrei Zhdanov, landed the supremacy of Soviet culture and urged an offensive against the 'decadent' Western world. In an admonition to Soviet writers Zhdanov said:

Is it right for Soviet patriots like us, representatives of progressive Soviet culture, to play the part of admirers or disciples of bourgeois culture? Our literature reflects a society which is on a higher plane than any bourgeois culture and therefore, it need hardly be said, has the right to teach others the new, universal morals.[7]

(It should be pointed out that here, as on other occasions, the word 'Soviet' is conveniently ambiguous: for 'Soviet' one can read 'socialist' or 'Russian'.)

As a consequence, approximate Russian equivalents were invented to replace English soccer terms: *futbol* was to become *nozhnoi myach*, *offside* – *vne igry*, *goalkeeper* – *vratar*, *corner* – *uglovoi*, *pass* – *podacha*, *forvard* – *napadayuschchy*, *bootsy* – *botinki*, *shorty* – *trusiki* and, ironically enough, *penalty* – *shtrafnoi* (from the German *Straf*). It is interesting to note that at a Soviet soccer match today one can hear a mixture of all these terms (often used by the same person), although *nozhnoi myach* never caught on, unlike *ruchnoi myach* (handball) which competes in current usage with *gandbol*.

Since the war Soviet performance in world soccer has had mixed success. When the Soviet national team made its debut at the 1952 Olympics it lost to Yugoslavia in the quarter finals, but it won the 1956 Olympic soccer tourney. Despite the fact that Dinamo Kiev won the European Cupwinners' Cup and then the Champions' Cup in 1975, Soviet club sides have not done as well as English, Scottish, West German or Dutch teams in international tournaments. And, like England, the USSR failed to qualify for the 1974 and 1978 World Cup finals. Although soccer has been regarded, therefore, as an effective means of competing peacefully with the West, it has not been a sport in which to observe the superiority of the Soviet system.

## Contemporary Problems

Over the last two decades the pressures on clubs and players to be successful have steadily built up. Training schedules have been intensified, previously weak teams beyond the capital (especially those in non-Russian areas) have risen to prominence, and problems associated with professional soccer in the West – unruly crowds, rough play, illegal practices and corruption – have grown apace. Some of the problems have accompanied Soviet soccer since the organization of club competition in the early years. But the extent of the problem is relatively new; so, too, are the vigorous attempts by the authorities to see that 'the norms of Soviet living' are upheld. Examples of malpractice have received wide publicity in the Soviet Press (from which my material is wholly taken), and the seamier side of soccer has by no means been hidden from the public gaze.

A growing problem is that of 'pampered' players. A 'master' footballer – that is, one who devotes more or less all of his time to training for and playing soccer during his active career – is paid by his sports society according to his sports ranking and certain other considerations, so that he can devote a great deal of his time to sport and can be coached under the auspices of, and use the facilities of, the society (such as Spartak, Dinamo, Torpedo, Lokomotiv). As an example of payment (though details are never publicized, presumably for fear of charges that payments contravene Olympic rules), a player in the top national league would receive a basic salary from the sports society of 180 rubles a month. If he has a Master of Sport ranking or has represented his country, he will receive another thirty or forty rubles respectively, a bonus that is paid to him by the USSR Sports Committee. Additionally, he is likely to receive unofficial payments from various organizations associated with his sports society or town team as bonuses for team success and for playing extra matches outside the normal league and cup programme. Players for Moscow Spartak, for example, would receive undercover bonus payments for winning matches against such organizations as the Moscow City Soviet, whose employees are members of the Spartak trade union sports society. A player's utility value may also secure for him certain perquisites, such as a good apartment or a car.

The authorities have, on the whole, turned a blind eye to such illegal payments as long as they remained within 'reasonable' limits. However, the extremes to which this bonus system can lead are clearly a cause for heart-searching. The worst examples would seem to have concerned the 1st Division club Odessa Chornomorets, which ten years ago received a million-ruble training camp paid for by the Odessa Steamship Line; the Line also paid out between 2000 and 3000 rubles each to five players in the team over a period of four months during 1970. Another 50,000 rubles came as a 'financial stimulus' to the team from the Odessa Port Authority. Factories in the city provided other inducements. The club itself provided players with well furnished flats, cars and 'pocket-money', particularly to attract good players from other clubs. Several state organizations, including the local police, were aware of these misdemeanours but ignored them. Similar scandals were exposed in regard to the Azerbaidzhan soccer team Neftchi (also at the time in Division 1), whose players were involved in drunken brawls in public and misconduct on the field, including an assault on match officials.

As the Chornomorets and Neftchi investigations revealed, many top-class soccer clubs are 'supported' by wealthy patrons, who grant players financial inducements for winning. Some top teams have even been accused of 'fixing' the result of a match if the price is right: it was reported in the Soviet Press in 1977 that results had been 'fixed' in games between Divison 1 teams Kiev Dinamo and Leningrad Zenit, and between Division 2 teams Moscow Lokomotiv and Zarya Voroshilovgrad.

The punishment for such offences varies considerably: some teams and players have been demoted or debarred from competition; some footballers have been imprisoned and others fined or held up to public censure in the Press. However, it is also evident that in a number of instances sentences have not been carried out. Such is the premium that some put on winning.

Apart from official punishment meted out to individuals, two methods of tackling the misconduct problem may merit attention elsewhere. First, the team manager is held responsible for the conduct of his players on and off the field. Recently the team manager of the Georgian team Guria was dismissed for neglecting his educational duties – the team captain had consistently failed to thank match officials after matches. All clubs are also supposed to have a full-time official (sometimes one of the players) who is responsible for the moral behaviour of everyone associated with the club; this job is sometimes combined with the post of Komsomol secretary for the team. Second, an innovation recently introduced to tackle the mounting problems is the annual post-season seminar on the state of Soviet football. team managers, coaches, players, referees and sports writers all take part.

Rough play and crowd trouble have prompted lively comment and official action in recent years. The problem seems to be growing: twenty players were sent off in first-class matches during the 1970 season; eleven were sent off and 163 booked in 1971; but there were as many as 291 cautions and sendings off in Division 1 alone in the 1976 season. Official concern is said to be considerable because such rough play and discourtesy to match officials and the opposing team evidently stem from the 'victory at all costs' mentality, which 'is contrary to Soviet ethics and presents a bad example to young people'.[8] It was recently recalled that the old Anglo–German club Victoria, which played in St Petersburg before the Revolution, had as its motto 'Lose with Honour', and that Stanley Matthews did not receive a single booking in his long career: 'These were the models to follow.'[9]

The mounting problem of unruly conduct on the pitch is being matched by that among spectators. Soviet soccer fans are no less prone to misbehaviour than their counterparts in some Western countries although they have not reached the stage of whirling rattles, shaking flags, singing abusive songs, throwing stones, bottles, darts and beer cans at opposing fans and players – actions which, needless to say, would be very much discouraged by the Soviet authorities. Nevertheless, over the years Soviet soccer grounds, where spectators sit for the match, have come to enjoy a reputation as locations for festivities not altogether connected with sport. A campaign was launched in 1972 to prevent the sale of alcohol at soccer stadiums and to see that no spirits were brought into matches (wine and beer are permissible). All the same, the problems of drunkenness and violence persist. A soccer fan was sentenced to death for fatally stabbing a youth during a match in Kiev in 1973; after another match in the Ukraine, 'a hooligan hit a Lipetsk player over the head with a hard object wrapped in paper'. Several instances have been reported of confrontations between fans of rival nationalities, involving particularly Georgians and Azerbaidzhanians. This is a problem that, in my view, will increase as supporters of national teams gain the time and money that will enable them to follow their teams about the country.

Such negative aspects of Soviet sport should not be exaggerated or sensationalized. The incidents mentioned above and publicized in the Soviet Press are isolated examples. There is nothing in the USSR to compare with the regular and sustained crowd problems of British soccer, partly because the state employs a number of controls and sanctions, deals quite severely with miscreants and does not permit its media to be charged with the sort of jingoism that awakens unrealistic expectations in the sporting public.

## Training

We have already noted the Soviet view that to do well in top-class sport, especially against foreign opposition, requires more or less full-time application. A promising footballer is therefore likely to be taken into one of the clubs in the Soviet soccer league, which consists of sixteen teams in Division 1, twenty-two teams in Division 2 and 126 teams in Division 3, divided into six geographical zones.

If a youngster wants to take up soccer seriously he would normally join a soccer section at a children's and young people's sports school, come under expert training, play for a team and move up systematically through the rankings. Boys are normally chosen at 9 or 10 and taken into the preparatory or junior group. Training takes place at the end of the normal school day and extends over seven or eight years; the club usually has four practice sessions of up to two hours and one game a week in a district or city league for each of its charges under the age of 16. At 16 and over the boys attend five times a week for three- and four-hour sessions.

All clubs in Divisions 1 and 2 have their own junior soccer schools with a full course of sports training for boys from about 10 onwards. Training with Division 3 clubs normally begins later, from 12 or 13, often because they do not have adequate training facilities or enough coaches to operate high-standard schools. In recent years some top clubs (Minsk Dinamo, for example) have reduced the age of entry to 7 or 8. The Minsk soccer school has been running since 1970 and 700 boys have enrolled; they train under qualified soccer coaches, several of them former Dinamo players. The school operates all the year round, with training indoors in winter on a full-size synthetic turf pitch. This example has been taken up (since 1977) by Moscow Dinamo as well, with the opening of their own indoor full-size pitch for winter training and competition.

Once a player is taken onto the staff of a senior club, he can devote his time to training and competition, although he is not free of the obligation to study for a higher qualification. It may be useful here to describe my personal experience when, in early 1970, I accompanied a Soviet friend (who was then an international footballer) to an institute of physical culture at which he had studied for five years. He assured me that nobody is permitted to play in Soviet league soccer without completing ten years of schooling; moreover, of the twenty-seven players attached to the permanent staff of his soccer club, twenty-four were studying then or had studied in higher education. On our way out of the institute, in fact, we met a group of footballers from three other clubs who were just arriving for evening classes. Although I have no doubt that the rules are sometimes bent, my impression that serious study is an essential part of an active footballer's life has subsequently been confirmed. The Soviet concern with further education among sportsmen contrasts most forcefully with the situation in most Western soccer clubs.

To sum up, soccer has been central to the development of the Soviet sports movement, as we have seen, and has played an important role in social development. The authorities have come to regard such team games as soccer as useful instruments through which to promote communication and understanding between them and the public; moreover, in a highly disciplined society they have endeavoured to satisfy the need for pleasurable excitement by providing it in a reasonably orderly, relatively harmless way, without the gross excesses that have marked the game in some Western and developing states.

Despite the shortcomings of Soviet soccer a number of its features merit careful examination – the career training provided for active players, the junior soccer schools, sober reporting in the mass media, annual seminars, methods of crowd control. At the same time, the USSR might benefit from considering Western experience in such areas as the wide provision of public pitches and facilities for casual players, self-organization among many local clubs and leagues and training methods in the more successful soccer clubs. The exchange of experience in soccer, as in other sports, would undoubtedly be of mutual benefit.

## NOTES

[1] *Sport*, 16 October 1903, p. 19.
[2] *Giants Cast Long Shadows* (London, 1958), pp. 173–4.
[3] *Vestnik fizicheskoi kul'tury*, No. 3, 1927, p. 7.
[4] A. Ekart, *Vanished without Trace* (London, 1954), p. 188.
[5] *Ibid.*
[6] *Povest' o futbole* (Moscow, 1973), p. 168.
[7] *Pravda*, 6 June 1946, p. 1.
[8] *Sovetsky sport*, 13 May 1971, p. 30.
[9] *Sport v SSSR*, No. 6, 1970, p. 12.

Chapter 8

# Women and Sport

Followers of Western sports reporting on Soviet sportswomen may well be forgiven for thinking that Russian and
other East European women who go in for sport are generally unfeminine, look old before their time, have to be
trained to smile and possess doubtful sexual inclinations.
Worse, their huge proportions often scare the pants off
some Western males brought up to regard their women as
ideally weak in head and arm, submissive and nubile.
Women, like sport and the men who write about both, are,
of course, socially conditioned and can properly be understood only in relation to the society that begets them.

There is no space here to pronounce adequately on
Soviet women and sport, on how they came to attain their
present position or even on how they interact. I am concerned simply to describe in this chapter certain aspects of
women in sport in the USSR today which contribute to our
picture of Soviet sport as a background to the Olympics.

## Some Signal Achievements

To start with the most positive aspects of Soviet women
and sport, it has to be said that today more or less equal
amounts of time and money are devoted to sport for men
and women in Soviet schools, colleges and the sports
societies. Soviet women are able to pursue a wide range of

sports that present no threat to their femininity, and in sports periodicals roughly equal space is devoted to sportsmen and sportswomen.

Soviet girls who show talent in sport are encouraged to develop this talent free of charge at one of the children's and young people's sports schools. In 1974 of the 1,737,900 children attending such schools, 584,800 (that is, just over a third) were girls. Girls also have approximately equal access to the sports boarding schools.

Soviet girls make up an overwhelming majority not only of teachers of physical education in schools, but also of graduates in sport and physical education generally. In the 1971–2 academic year 56 per cent of such students were women, and of all the physical education graduates embarking on teaching careers, 87 per cent were women. Further, women make up 52,000 (well over a third) of the 141,000 full-time coaches and instructors in the USSR.

Although Soviet women's participation in sport is more restricted than the men's, there is almost no difference in the numbers of each sex who meet the standards and pass the tests in the nationwide fitness programme (GTO): in 1974 of the twelve million people who obtained their GTO badges, 5,090,000 were girls. Sportswomen seem to be accepted as performers in their own right within the Soviet sports movement, both among the population as a whole and among sports writers. It is significant that in a poll conducted among sports writers (presumably mostly men) to select the sports personality of 1973 from among fifty-five candidates representing twenty-seven sports, the top five places went to women, two of whom represented 'muscular' field sports:

1. Irina Rodnina (figure skating)
2. Ludmilla Turishcheva (gymnastics)
3. Faina Mel'nik (shot putt)
4. Galina Shugurova (modern gymnastics)

5. Nadezhda Chizhova (discus)
6. Valery Kharlamov (ice hockey)
7. Pavel Pervukhin (weightlifting)
8. Levon Tediashvili (wrestling)
9. Pavel Lednev (pentathlon)
10. Anatoly Karpov (chess)

Soviet sportswomen have been accorded a great deal of respect as a result of the success they have gained for their country in international sport, and this has helped to enhance their social standing in society. As a Soviet writer has put it, 'Sport is a major area in which women have been able to succeed and, through their success, achieve greater social recognition in the wider society.'[1] It is noteworthy that Soviet women not only make up a sizeable proportion of USSR teams in multi-sport international tournaments, but they also make an important, sometimes decisive, contribution to the success of the USSR overall. Thus, in the fourteen athletics matches held between the USSR and the USA between 1958 and 1976 the USSR amassed the higher aggregate total of medals and points twelve times; but Soviet men won only four times and *Soviet women lost only once*. In other words, if it were not for Soviet women, the USSR would have lost most matches. To give another example, Soviet women comprised just over a third of the Soviet contingent to the 1976 Montreal Olympics (although women competed in only forty-nine of the 186 events – almost a sixth), winning thirty-six of the 125 Soviet medals. The East German example is even more striking: women made up 40 per cent of the GDR team and won more than half the team's gold and silver medals. By contrast, American women made up a quarter, British and West German women just over a fifth and French women less than a fifth of their respective teams. In the 1976 Winter Olympics Soviet women contributed sixteen of the twenty-seven USSR medals.

*Faina Mel'nik, Olympic champion shot-putter. Participation in*
*'muscular' sports is not seen as incongruent with notions of desirable*
*feminine demeanour*

Besides reflecting the attention given in the USSR to
women's sport, the Soviet women's contribution to the
overall success of the USSR is clearly of some significance
internationally. Women outside the USSR have been able
to quote the Soviet example when trying to gain admission
to sports and sporting institutions that men had previously
regarded as their preserve, and to play upon national pride
in urging that their countries be given a chance to excel.
Moreover, the grace, skill and strength displayed by Soviet
sportswomen in a whole range of sports has inspired many
young women in other parts of the world to take up a sport
they would otherwise have spurned. In her opening

address to the first Canadian national conference on women and sport in May 1974 the eminent Canadian physical educationalist Laura Sabia pointed to the example of Soviet women:

I don't know whether you are impressed, but I am, very much so, with the gymnastics that I have seen of the young Russian ladies. they were symphonies of the most beautiful music I have ever seen. Their bodies glowed with activity and serenity and with beauty untold. It was absolutely fantastic. These girls must have put untold hours, and hours of frustration too, into developing the skills that they have acquired. Now this is something else we have to instil in our young girls.

The list of achievements of Soviet sportswomen is long and imposing, especially when compared with those of women in the more 'advanced' and 'democratic' nations of the West. All the same, the picture would be neither complete nor fair to Soviet women if a number of problems were ignored – some of which are examined below.

*Participation in Sport among Soviet Men and Women*

A discrepancy exists between men and women in all sections of Soviet society where participation in sport – and the use of free time generally – is concerned. Several social surveys have attested to this discrepancy; three are mentioned below.

In a time budget survey, the results of which were published in 1972, weekly time spent on sport, physical culture and outdoor recreation averaged 30 minutes for unmarried girls, 5 minutes for newly married girls, 25 minutes for married women with a small family, 5 minutes for married women with more than two children and 10 minutes for women over 40. The figures for men were 1 hour 55 minutes, 1 hour 50 minutes and 1 hour 25 minutes respectively. Figures for men over 40 were unavailable. On average, therefore, men spent five times more time on sport and recreation than women.

In another survey published in the same year women working a five- or six-day week spent 2 per cent of their spare time on regular sporting activities and 9 per cent on casual sport ('now and again'). Men, on the other hand, devoted 7 per cent of their free time to regular sport and 22 per cent to casual sport in a five-day week, and in a six-day week 5 per cent and 21 per cent respectively. On average, then, men spent at least three times more time on sport than women.

A third survey, conducted at factories in the Tartar capital of Kazan and published in 1975, indicated that women devoted between 2 and 2.5 times less time on sport than men. An earlier study, published in 1967, discovered that men spent 1.2 times more time than women on social activities, self-improvement and outdoor recreation, 1.7 times more time on study, 2.2 times more time on sport and 4 times more time on hobbies. It would appear, therefore, that after all their chores Soviet women do not have a great deal of time left for sport and certainly have less than men to spend on recreation.

Despite this disparity, it is a persistent theme in Soviet writing on women's emancipation that they should be drawn more into sporting activities. There seems little doubt that the situation has improved over the last twenty years. In 1959 only 5.6 per cent of the female population went in for sport on any regular and organized basis; by 1967 women who regularly pursued an organized sport made up 14.1 per cent of the female population (by contrast with sporting males, who made up 37 per cent of the male population). Further, in 1975 women comprised 35 per cent of the total number of registered members of sports societies attending sports sessions no less than twice a week over a six-month period.

*Women's Sport in Former Muslim Areas*

It is noticeable that the lowest figures for women's participation in sport are those for the areas of Muslim culture,
while the highest figures are those for the most industrially
and culturally advanced areas, the three Baltic republics,
the Ukraine and Belorussia. Thus, whereas women constituted 40 per cent of all regular athletes in the population of
Belorrussia in 1975, 36 per cent in Estonia and Russia and 35
per cent in the Ukraine and Latvia, they made up only 33
per cent in Uzbekistan and Kirgizia, 32 per cent in
Kazakhstan, 25 per cent in Azerbaidzhan and Turkmenia
and 21 per cent in Tadzhikistan.

That old customs die hard, and that prejudice against
girls taking part at all in sport still exists, is confirmed by a
number of writers and surveys. A Kazakh author, writing
in 1973, agrees that 'some parents forbid their daughters to
dance and play a sport. This explains the difficulties
encountered in trying to train ballerinas, gymnasts, volleyball players, etc., in Kazakhstan.'[2] Uzbek authors attri-
bute the limited participation in sport of Uzbek girls partly
to the refusal of 'some parents to allow their daughters to
bare their arms and legs, so preventing them from pursuing
their favourite sport.'[3] Research into the sporting interests
of schoolchildren in the old Muslim city of Baku
(Azerbaidzhan) revealed that 'vestiges of the past exist in
the attitudes of many parents who disapprove of their
children, especially girls, practising sport.' It was found
that the share of sportswomen in Azerbaidzhanian teams
competing in the *spartakiads* has rarely risen above 10 per
cent: 12.9 per cent in 1956, 10.1 per cent in 1959 and 1963,
7.5 per cent in 1967 and 9.5 per cent in 1971.

Evidently, women's participation in sport in an erstwhile
socially backward Muslim area (where women were effectively excluded from all public life some fifty years ago) has
assisted them to gain some measure of emancipation. The

Chairman of the Uzbek Parliamentary Committee on Youth Affairs has said that 'in Uzbekistan, as in other Central Asian republics, the women's path to sport has been linked with a struggle against religious prejudices and for equal status in society.' Such events as the First *Spartakiad* for Rural Women of Uzbekistan in 1969 (with 300 finalists, three-quarters of whom were of Uzbek nationality) are conscious attempts to draw Central Asian women into sport as one means of furthering their social progress. As was mentioned in a reference to women in Central Asia at a Soviet conference in 1975 on women and sport, 'physical culture has become an effective and visible means of combating religious prejudices and reactionary traditions of the old way of life; it has played a certain part in removing the spiritual oppression of women and in fighting for a new and happy life.'

*Conflicting Views on Women and Sport*

While there seems to be little or no disagreement among Soviet writers about the desirability of women taking part in sport in general, there has certainly been no coherent policy in regard to which sports women should be encouraged to take up. In the early years of the Revolution and before the last war, there appear to have been few inhibitions about women taking up any sport, including soccer and ice hockey. Particularly in recent years, however, conflicting opinions have appeared in the Press, and some official measures have been taken to discourage women's participation in certain sports. This came to a head in 1973 when the USSR Sports Committee adopted a resolution which contained specific recommendations for women's sport and stimulated discussion of biological differences and women's alleged predisposition for certain sports. The main thrust of the official argument was that women should not engage in sports that were contra-indicated, harmful or morally degrading (according to the official view of femininity). Such 'perverse' activities included women's soccer and wrestling.

In regard to women's soccer, it would appear that several teams had sprung up mainly in the Ukraine in the early 1970s which had played both within and outside the republic. This activity was criticized for two reasons: first, 'the principal aim was for certain sports administrators to obtain additional income through the unhealthy interest shown by some male spectators in women's soccer matches.' This was also the theme of an article in the satirical magazine *Krokodil*, following a women's soccer match in Sochi in 1972. The match was a sell-out and put on 'obviously to right the stadium's financial affairs'. Second, 'women's soccer may damage sexual functions and may cause varicose veins, thrombophlebitis, etc.'

The confusion over women's soccer is illustrated by the fact that official discouragement had been preceded by some positive comments in the Press on women's soccer abroad, including in Eastern Europe. Moreover, the resolution did not ban soccer for women; it only discouraged sports organizations from arranging matches. It is likely that the sport will develop in future years when the present climate has altered. It may be recalled that women's soccer developed in the West initially as commercial entertainment (titillation) for men, but eventually shed this mantle when women became skilful at the game (and therefore far less interesting as curiosities).

Like women's soccer, wrestling (the Soviet 'unarmed combat' version, *sambo*) was condemned because it had been 'exploited by "sports businessmen" and turned into "strength-and-beauty" contests that were degrading to Soviet womanhood'.[4] One can understand the official disquiet at women's wrestling or judo matches arranged as public spectacles, given the ideological objections to hedonistic sex in general, public sexuality, deviations from straight marital intercourse and commercial exploitation. Henceforth, women's *sambo* was permitted only when confined to non-competitive events under the supervision of the civil defence organization DOSAAF or the Ministry of the Interior's sports organization, Dinamo.

These measures provoked a number of statements from medical men and educationalists 'justifying' the resolution and laying down guidelines for women's sport. It was said, for example, that biological differences affect women's rate of participation, levels of performance and skills in certain sports. Thus

with training, the functional potential of the female organism increases considerably and approximates in some indices to that of the male. Nevertheless, the level of performance of women is no more than 70–80 per cent of that of men.[5]

It would follow that

women are more suited to sports which develop speed, skill, plasticity, co-ordination and grace of movement – such as gymnastics, modern gymnastics, figure skating, swimming, athletics, fencing and certain team sports. Women's health is also enhanced by such sports as speed skating, skiing and shooting.[6]

Another male writer made the contentious point that

in choosing a sport, girls are motivated by a beautiful figure, grace and suppleness, boys by strength, stamina, skill and speed.[7]

None of the authors defended the right of women to take up whatever sport they wished; on the other hand, no one suggested that they should be prevented from pursuing the sport of their choice, even if it were selected from among those officially discredited.

*Some Conclusions*

Soviet women have less free time than men and show lower rates of participation and levels of performance, although the gap is narrowing steadily. They appear to be more sporting than their Western counterparts and receive much official encouragement to be so. In a survey sponsored by UNESCO (published in 1967) into time expenditure across ten nations, it was found that 11.4 per cent of all working women and 15.4 per cent of non-working women participated regularly in sport in the USSR, by comparison with participation rates of 4.1 and 4.7 per cent for the USA, 2.1 and 1.4 per cent for France, and 5.4 and 5.2 per cent for West Germany respectively. Although the difficulties associated with making valid comparisons warn against drawing far-reaching conclusions from this survey, the Soviet figures coincide with those given earlier, and there is no doubt that the sporting woman is a positive heroine in Soviet society – an ideal to which all women are urged to aspire.

The reasons for official encouragement of women to engage in sport, including physically exacting and 'muscular' activities, have to be sought in the Soviet State's political and material needs as well as in its ideology. These may be assumed to include the following areas of concern.

THE ECONOMY

The work of women has been vital to economic development – and sport is thought to help make workers disciplined, physically fit and mentally alert. The role of women in the Soviet economy was extended by the shortfall of men in the population after the last war. Given the economic necessity for women to engage in physically exhausting jobs (as, for example, road mending and house building), the physical and psychological qualities required for, or developed by, successful participation in sport are not incongruent with notions about the 'essential nature of femininity' and desirable feminine demeanour (as perceived in Soviet conditions). Physical vigour and competitiveness – which are often considered 'masculine' qualities in the West – remain compatible with the ways in which women are expected to present themselves in everyday life and with the various occupational roles and identities which are available to them in society.

## DEFENCE

Women have been essential to the country's defence and military preparedness, and physical training through sport (particularly as women are exempt from peacetime military service) is, again, thought to be the best way to prepare them for these.

## INTERNATIONAL PRESTIGE

Not only has sport proved (since the last war) to be an effective means by which the Soviet Union may compete peacefully with the West – and often demonstrate in practice the 'superiority of the socialist system' – but it has also been used to generate popular sentiments of friendship towards the USSR (especially in developing and neutral states) and to smooth the way to proffered aid and treaty relations. We have already noted the vital part played by Soviet sportswomen in helping the USSR to attain these goals.

SOCIAL CHANGE

The Soviet authorities have used sport as a vehicle for that type of women's emancipation officially desired in the USSR. The fact that women display courage, grace and intellectual and physical skills in the sporting arena, win prestige for club and country, factory and farm, region and ethnic group, and combine with men to compete in national and international contests has done much for their social status, particularly in the old Muslim-dominated areas.

The treats to femininity that sports are deemed to present in the West seem to have been countered to a considerable extent in the USSR. Most significantly, women's sporting achievements have both reflected and reinforced processes of change in the role and status of women in Soviet society. There are lessons to be learnt here not only for the women's movement in advanced Western countries but also for policy makers in all modernizing societies.

## NOTES

[1] *Sport v SSSR*, No. 3, 1975, p. 1.
[2] N. S. Sarsenbaev, *Obychai, traditsii i obshchestvennaya zhizn'* (Alma Ata, 1974), p. 157.
[3] Yu. V. Borisov, *Planirovanie razvitiya fizicheskoi kul'tury i sporta sredi sel'skovo naseleniya* (Moscow, 1974), p. 85.
[4] *Teoriya i praktika fizicheskoi kul'tury*, No. 10, 1973, p. 62.
[5] *Sovetsky sport*, 25 January 1973, p. 3.
[6] I. I. Pereverzin, *Prognozirovanie i planirovanie fizicheskoi kul'tury* (Moscow, 1972), pp. 16–17.
[7] *Ibid.*

Chapter 9

# The Olympic Games

Russia was a founding member of the modern Olympic movement and Russian sportsmen first participated in the Olympic Games in 1908 (the Fourth Olympics, held in London). A team of five contestants went to Britain, sponsored by voluntary contributions. It did surprisingly well, winning a gold medal in figure skating, two silvers in wrestling and taking fourteenth place overall (among twenty-two nations). For the next Olympics, held in Stockholm in 1912, the Russian sports societies were prepared to sponsor a much larger contingent. The government, recognizing the prestige value of sports success as a prop for their ailing regime, set up a Russian Olympic Committee headed by Baron F. Meyendorf. With quite generous government backing and organization, a team of 169 athletes gathered to take part in fifteen sports on the Olympic programme. Whether the prospects of a foreign jaunt were too intoxicating (notably to the army officers, who made up over half the party) is uncertain, but many of the team (including Baron Meyendorf) missed the boat altogether and had to stay behind. In the Games Russia ultimately shared fifteen place with Austria (out of twenty-eight) and won few medals. The best performance was that of a wrestler, M. Klein, who, in spite of having broken his arm in the semi-final and having to forfeit his chance to wrestle in the final, won a silver medal. The only other medals were one in gymnastics, second place for the Russian team in pistol and revolver shooting and third places in yachting and clay pigeon shooting. The Olympic setback was a reflection of the backward state of Russian sport and Russian society.

Although it was to be another forty years before Russia returned to the Olympic movement, the International Olympic Committee continued forlornly to recognize the old Russian Olympic Committee for several years after the 1917 Revolution, and such notables as Prince Urusov, Count Ribopierre, Baron Villebrand and General Butovsky all served on the International Committee in the period up to 1932.

*Promoting World Revolution after 1917*

On the assumption that world revolution was not far distant and that until then the world would be split irreconcilably into two hostile camps, the Soviet authorities after 1917 at first ignored 'bourgeois' sports organizations, refused to affiliate to their international federations and boycotted their competitions, especially the Olympic Games, which were characterized as designed 'to deflect the workers from the class struggle while training them for new imperialist wars'. The Declaration on the Formation of the USSR, adopted on 30 December 1922, stated clearly the fundamental ideas of the Soviet leaders in international affairs: 'Since the formation of the Soviet republics, the states of the world have been split into two camps: the camp of capitalism and the camp of socialism . . . The USSR is to serve as a decisive new step on the way to uniting the workers of the world into a World Socialist Republic.' The spreading of communism throughout the world was regarded not simply as an ideological precept, but as a practical necessity, on which depended the very survival of the Soviet state.

Initially then, excursions beyond Soviet borders were

almost entirely confined to competitions with foreign workers' teams, like the Finnish Labour Team TUL and the team of the French communist trade union CFGT. As the 1920s wore on, the USSRs need for peaceful coexistence (especially with the her neighbours), a desire to compete against the world's best teams and the consideration that the bourgeoisie in certain backward states were playing a progressive role stimulated some limited contacts. For the most part, however, as long as the USSR remained isolated and weak internationally, foreign sports relations were restricted to workers' sports organizations and reflected the policy of the Communist International (Comintern).[1] Soviet foreign sports policy was, in fact, largely identical with and conducted through the International Association of Red Sports and Gymnastics Organizations, better known as Red Sport International (RSI). The RSI was formed at the First International Congress of representatives of revolutionary workers' sports organizations in July 1921; the founder members were workers' sports organizations from eight countries: Czechoslovakia, Finland, France, Germany, Hungary, Italy, Soviet Russia and Sweden (by 1924 the USA, Norway and Uruguay were also represented).

One of the actions of the RSI was to arrange workers' Olympics the first of which, held in Moscow in 1928, were designed to demonstrate proletarian internationalism in sport and to counterbalance the bourgeois Olympics being held the same year in Paris. Although the Moscow Olympics were dominated by Soviet athletes, a sizeable foreign contingent arrived: some 600 foreign athletes from a dozen or more countries including Britain, France, Germany and Sweden. The programme included twenty-one sports, approximating to the programme of the 'bourgeois' Olympics. It differed from the latter, however, in that, besides team and individual competitions, it contained a variety of pageants and displays, including elaborate opening and closing ceremonies, carnivals, mass games, and car and motorcycle rallies. There were also displays of folk games and folk dancing and of team games that were unfamiliar to many of the participants (for example, rugby, tennis, field hockey), as well as mock battles between the 'world proletariat' and 'world bourgeoisie'.

Such was the Soviet policy in sport, in brief, prior to World War II.

## The USSR as a World Power

With the radical change in the world balance of power that followed the Allied victory in the war, Soviet policy in regard to international sport changed too. At first Soviet sportsmen moved cautiously into international competition. No Soviet team was sent to the London Olympic Games of 1948; instead a number of officials attended the Games as observers. Only in April 1951 was a Soviet Olympic Committee formed and, in May, accepted by the IOC.

The USSR made its Olympic debut at the fifteenth Olympic Games, held in Helsinki in 1952. The extent of Soviet preparation was evident from the fact that Soviet athletes contested all events in the Olympic programme (with the exception of field hockey). In view of the fact that hardly any of the Soviet athletes had competed previously against world-class opposition from outside the USSR, the Soviet performance was remarkable. Although according to the unofficial Olympic table (see Table 6) the USSR gained fewer gold medals than the USA (22:40), it gained more silver (30:19) and bronze (19:17) and tied with the USA in points allotted for the first six places (according to the system used in the *Olympic Bulletin*).

The USSR took no part in the 1952 Winter Olympics and made its winter debut only in 1956 at Cortina D'Ampezzo in

Table 6

*Soviet performance in the Olympic Games 1952–76*

| Year | Summer Games | | | | | | Winter Games | | | | | |
|---|---|---|---|---|---|---|---|---|---|---|---|---|
| | | | | | Nearest rival | | | | | | Nearest rival | |
| | Gold medals | Medal total[h] | Points[a] | Position | Medals | Points[a] | Gold medals | Medal total | Points[a] | Position | Medals | Points[a] |
| 1952 | 22 | 71 | 494 | 1 | 76 | 494[c] | –[b] | –[b] | –[b] | –[b] | –[b] | –[b] |
| 1956 | 37 | 98 | 624.5 | 1 | 74 | 498[c] | 7 | 16 | 103 | 1 | 11 | 66.5[d] |
| 1960 | 43 | 103 | 683 | 1 | 71 | 463.5[c] | 7 | 21 | 146.5 | 1 | 7 | 62.5[e] |
| 1964 | 30 | 96 | 608.3 | 1 | 90 | 581.8[c] | 11 | 25 | 183 | 1 | 15 | 89.3[f] |
| 1968 | 29 | 91 | 591.5 | 2 | 106 | 709[c] | 5 | 13 | 92 | 2 | 14 | 103[f] |
| 1972 | 50 | 99 | 665.5 | 1 | 93 | 636.5[c] | 8 | 16 | 120 | 1 | 14 | 83[g] |
| 1976 | 47 | 125 | 788.5 | 1 | 90 | 636.5[g] | 13 | 27 | 201 | 1 | 19 | 138[g] |

[a] The points allocation is that used in the *Olympic Bulletin*: awarding seven points for first place, five for second and so on down to one point for sixth place.
[b] USSR not participating.
[h] The comparative British medal totals for the Summer Olympics were: 1952–11, 1956–24, 1960–20, 1964–18, 1968–13, 1972–18, 1976–13.
[c] USA.     [d] Austria.     [e] Sweden.     [f] Norway.     [g] East Germany.

*Sources:* K. A. Andrianov et al. (eds.), *Olimpiiskie igry* (Moscow, 1970); *Sovetsky sport*, 16 February 1972, p. 4; *Sportsworld*, September 1972; *Sport v SSSR*, No. 3, 1976, p. i; *The Times*, 2 August 1976, p. 8.

Italy. There it amassed more medals and points than any other competitor, winning gold medals in speed skating, skiing and ice hockey. The ice hockey success was particularly creditable, since the sport had only been taken up in the Soviet Union after the war; two years before the 1956 Olympics the Soviet ice hockey team had won the World Championships at its first attempt.

At the next Olympics, held in Melbourne in 1956, the USSR sent a team of over 300 athletes. Once again, all events except field hockey were contested, and this time the scope of the challenge was much wider; besides gaining more medals and points than any other nation in the history of the Olympics, the USSR reaped its first gold medals in track events (both won by the late Vladimir Kuts), boxing, football, sculling, canoeing and the modern pentathlon.

There was no mistaking the boost that Olympic success gave at the time to the Soviet people's pride in their sportsmen. Nor were Soviet leaders slow to appreciate the benefit the USSR could derive from its enhanced reputation at home and abroad. By a decree of the USSR Supreme Soviet of 27 April 1957 a large group of Soviet athletes, coaches and sports officials were rewarded with some of the country's highest honours. As many as twenty-seven beneficiaries received the supreme honour: the Order of Lenin. Never before or since have the efforts of Soviet sportsmen been honoured so highly.

At the 1960 Olympic Games, held in winter at Squaw valley in the USA and in the summer in Rome, the USSR produced by far the most successful performance. In the winter it won three times as many medals as its nearest rival (Sweden). In the summer events it gained 103 medals (its nearest rival was the USA with seventy-one). Victories were recorded in sports comparatively new to the Soviet Union, like cycling, yachting, fencing and show jumping.

*Yachting at the Olympic venue of Tallinn on the Baltic Sea. Not a sport of the rich in the USSR*

In the following Olympic Games, held in the winter at Innsbruck in Austria and in the summer of 1964 in Tokyo, the USSR once more emerged triumphant. First gold medals were won in pairs figure skating (Belousova and Protopopov) and in the biathlon in the Winter Olympics, and Soviet contestants came first in seven out of the twenty-three sports in the summer programme: Greco-Roman Wrestling, weightlifting, boxing, gymnastics, fencing, the modern pentathlon and, for the first time, men's volleyball. A first gold medal was also won in swimming.

At the 1968 Olympics, however, the Soviet winter and summer contingents showed they were not invincible; the

USSR was placed second to Norway in the Winter Olympics, held at Grenoble in France, and second to the USA in the Summer Olympics, held in Mexico City.

In the winter and summer Olympic Games held during 1972 at Sapporo (Japan) and Munich (West Germany), the USSR reclaimed its leading position. In summer it acquired more gold medals and points than any nation had done before – this despite the obvious improvements in worldwide athletic standards, particularly in Eastern Europe and the Third World. Soviet success was achieved largely at the expense of the more established sports nations, primarily the USA. The spread of Soviet performance and success in the 1972 Summer Olympics confirmed that the USSR was the best all-round and most successful nation at the Games. It won nine of the twenty-three sports in which it competed, coming second in six sports and third in two sports; by comparison the USA had four firsts, three seconds and one third. Besides being superior overall, the USSR was also the most consistently versatile nation, being placed among the first six in twenty-three of the twenty-four sports in the Games (the USA achieved similar ranking in fourteen sports, East Germany in twelve, West Germany in nine). Commenting on the success of the USSR and other socialist states, a Soviet sports journal noted that 'the mounting influence of socialist sport on the world sports movement is one of the best and most comprehensible means of explaining to people throughout the world the advantages which the socialist system has over capitalism.'[2] Once again, in recognition of Soviet success, athletes, coaches and officials who had contributed to the Soviet victory were honoured (253 in all); six persons received the Order of Lenin, including Borzov, winner of the 100 metre and 200 metre sprints; Alexeyev, winner of the superheavy weightlifting division; and Saneyev, winner of the triple jump for the third Olympics in succession.

In the 1976 Montreal Olympics, the USSR once again provided the most outstanding performance in the history of the Games. Soviet athletes won medals in nineteen of the twenty-one sports, coming first in eight sports, second in seven, and third in four. Of the 430 Soviet athletes in the Olympics, as many as 259 won medals. This time a total of 347 Olympic athletes, coaches and officials received honours. Altogether, the USSR and the other socialist countries aggregated 121 gold medals out of 198.

All these results suggest that the Soviet Union has come a considerable way towards achieving its aim of world supremacy in sport.

The USSR appears to be most successful in the combat sports (wrestling, weightlifting, judo), the sports that call on *artistic expression* (gymnastics, figure skating and ice dancing), quasi-military sports (fencing, shooting, archery, biathlon, modern pentathlon, skiing and equestrian sports) and games that demand cerebral skills (chess and draughts). Albeit harnessed to a purposeful planning system, these skills may have their roots in the physical strength of the Slav peasant and belligerent border peoples like the Cossacks and Transcaucasians (Georgians, Armenians, Azerbaidzhanians), who produce many of the weightlifters, wrestlers and boxers; in the artistic sense of a people keenly appreciative of aesthetic self-expression in ballet and folk music; in the long-established association between sport and military training; and in the esteem in which Soviet society holds intellectual and cultural activities. The USSR is less successful in swimming, field and track events, and in sports like field hockey, rugby, badminton and tennis, which are relatively recent introductions. Its failure to dominate in these areas may be attributed partly to its climate and partly to the paucity of amenities generally – school playing fields, tennis courts, indoor stadiums and swimming pools above all. The international success in, and popular following for,

*World superheavy weightlifting champion Vasily Alexeyev*

team sports in the USSR may be due to the official encouragement given to them for the benefits they are felt to impart. Discipline, reliance on others and the merging of the individual with the group have long been valued by the Soviet authorities. It seems not unreasonable to suggest that the reasons for the popularity of team play and the international success of team sports may be sought in an environment that stresses team work and co-operation rather than individualism and self-interest.

*Sports Integration among Socialist Countries*

Soviet leaders have long regarded co-operation and mutual assistance in sport among socialist states as extremely important. There are two main reasons for this. The first is that sport is considered an efficacious means of advertising the advantages of socialism and demonstrating the superiority of the socialist way of life. It is felt that a sensible division of labour, the integration of effort and the support of the weak by the strong not only contribute to the improvement of all-round socialist performance, but also increase the influence of a united front of socialist countries in world forums. A leading sports administrator, D. I. Prokhorov, has written: 'The work of socialist sports organizations in the world sports movement is an integral part of the international ideological struggle.'[3] It is therefore regarded as important to increase the number of representatives of socialist states in international federations so as to 'democratize' them further and to help implant progressive policies. For these purposes, a standing committee of socialist countries was set up in 1974 to co-ordinate policy in international sports organizations.

The advance of socialist countries in the Olympic Games has been nothing short of remarkable and obviously owes much to this concerted effort. In 1952, when most of these nations made their Olympic debut, they accounted for 29 per cent of the medals; two decades later they took 47 per cent of the medals, and in 1976 as much as 57 per cent of the medal total. The *political* significance of this advance has often been stressed in the USSR; as Prokhorov has put it, 'The need for successful performances by athletes from socialist states is extremely important today; therefore the question of joint preparation has become vital both from the sporting *and from the political standpoint'* (my italics). [4]

The second major reason for sports integration among the socialist states is to create greater unity among them. In a book on international sport, A. O. Romanov has written that sports contacts 'help to strengthen fraternal co-operation and instil a sense of patriotism and international-ism among people from the socialist countries'. [5] From the Soviet point of view, this enables Soviet leaders to use sport to integrate the various socialist societies, to link them with Soviet institutions and policies and to maintain the USSR's 'vanguard' position within the socialist community. Re-lations have tended to reflect the political tenor of the bloc, with the Soviet Union defending (or, on occasion, impos-ing) its 'special relationship' as the 'most socialist state', and the other socialist states sometimes striving for com-pensatory supremacies that are denied them elsewhere. In the period 1948–56 most of the other socialist countries (Yugoslavia was a notable exception) were more or less obliged to learn from the Soviet model, to form Soviet-type administrative organizations and run physical-fitness pro-grammes like the GTO – this despite the long-standing sporting traditions of Hungary, Czechoslovakia (with its *Sokol* gymnastics) and East Germany, all of which had competed successfully in international sport many years before the USSR had begun to participate. The major sports associations set up in all the socialist countries (including Yugoslavia) were those based on the armed forces (TsSKA,

Honved, Legia, Red Star, Dukla and so on) and on the ministries for internal security (Dinamo). Although Soviet control of other sports systems has loosened since 1956, nonetheless major Soviet administrative changes normally herald similar changes elsewhere in Eastern Europe, as in 1959, when the Soviet sports societies were reorganized, and in 1968, when the present government-based Sports Committee was created.

Sports contacts between the socialist states embrace a variety of sports and take place at various levels. Athletes come together in such single-sport tournaments as the annual Peace cycle race across Eastern Europe and the Znamensky Brothers Memorial athletics meeting (held in Moscow), and in such multi-sport tournaments for specific groups and organizations as the Friendship sports tourneys for junior sportsmen, the socialist rural games, twinned-city games, the Baltic Sea Week and the annual sports meetings for the armed forces' and for the security forces' sports clubs.

The sporting aid given by the USSR and other socialist states to Cuba is an example of the process by which that country was drawn into the ambit of the socialist community after a period of isolation and hesitation. The immediate aim was to help harness and build up Cuban skill in order that Cuba might put up a good showing in sporting confrontations with other states on the American continent (Cuba subsequently came second to the USA in the 1972 Pan-American Games). Cuban successes in the Olympics and other tournaments provided ample means for linking sports success with the political system and for demonstrating to other Latin American states, through the popular and readily understandable medium of sport (which has particular appeal in Latin America), the advantages of the 'Cuban road to socialism'. Once Cuban sport was set on its feet, however, the foreign coaches and advisers withdrew, and Cuba is now, in turn, helping other socialist states, including the USSR and developing countries, in the field of sport.

More and more in recent years assistance has become a multilateral affair, with each socialist state giving the others help in its own specialist area. Thus, Bulgarian weightlifting coaches are sharing their experience within the bloc, as are Czechoslovak ice hockey coaches, Polish boxing coaches, Hungarian fencing, swimming and pentathlon coaches and East German swimming, athletics and skiing coaches. As a number of coaches in the socialist community build up specialized facilities and sports centres, they become increasingly able to gather together other sportsmen from within the bloc for joint training on the eve of important international events. Furthermore, a division of labour is developing in research too: Poland is specializing in the problems of sports management and outdoor recreation; Czechoslovakia in talent-spotting and sports testing; the USSR and German Democratic Republic in training methods. These and other forms of mutual assistance and integration are said to have become an important contributory factor in the international sporting successes of such states.

## Olympic Solidarity

The Soviet authorities have paid increasing attention to aid to the Third World in the field of sport, as well as in economic and in cultural spheres. This assistance takes the form of sending coaches and instructors abroad, building sports amenities, training foreign sports administrators in the Soviet Union, arranging tours and displays by Soviet Athletes and holding Sports Friendship Weeks that often have an overtly political character. Much of this aid, including the provision of sports amenities, is given free of charge. Sometimes sports contacts are used as a prelude to

*Lenin Stadium, central venue of the 1980 Olympics, as seen across the Moscow River from the University. Opened in 1956, it has seating for over 100,000 spectators*

political and other contacts. After all, as Romanov has stated, 'Sports ties are one way of establishing contacts between states even when diplomatic relations are absent.'[6]

In the twenty years up to 1978 over 600 Soviet coaches had worked in some forty African, Asian and Latin American countries. In late 1976 there were said to be more than 200 Soviet sports specialists working in thirty foreign states, and sports co-operation treaties had been signed with a number of Afro-Asian states. The USSR has built sports centres in many countries in Africa (Algeria, Congo, Senegal, Togo) and Asia (Afghanistan, Cambodia, Indonesia, Iraq), and students from thirty Afro-Asian states have received a Soviet coaching diploma. By 1977 some 250 persons from developing countries had graduated from Soviet institutes of physical culture; another 100 had completed dissertations in the field of sport and physical education at Soviet colleges.

Judging by the rapidly mounting scale of operations for promoting sport in developing nations, the Soviet leaders obviously regard sport as an important weapon in the 'battle for men's minds'. It is a serious business: 'The authority of sport in the world has grown enormously; there is no longer any place for dilettantism in the politics of sport.'[7] Given the signal successes of the USSR in international sport, such sporting aid is seen as an effective means of demonstrating the possibilities of the 'socialist path of development'. In organizing contacts and assistance, much emphasis is placed on the propaganda value of the successes attained in erstwhile backward areas in the Soviet Union: 'In arranging these contacts, we attach special importance to the sports organizations of the various republics, to sportsmen from Kazakhstan, Uzbekistan, Azerbaidzhan, Armenia and Georgia, when they visit Africa and Asia, and when the representatives of those countries meet our republican sportsmen at home.'[8]

It is noteworthy that, apart from individual visiting sportsmen, few Western states have given much officially sponsored sporting aid to developing countries. In fact, the pattern has generally been for promising 'colonial' athletes to be attracted away from their homelands to seek fame and fortune in the teams of metropolitan countries. Such a trend is particularly apparent in Italian, French and

Portuguese soccer (and, increasingly, in soccer in the USA) and in British cricket, boxing and athletics.

On final aspect of Soviet aid to Afro-Asian states has been support for Third World campaigns to exclude from international sport countries believed to be operating racial discrimination in sport. The Soviet Olympic Committee instigated moves in 1962 to exclude South Africa from the Olympic Games; the moves succeeded, and South Africa has subsequently not been able to compete in the Olympics. The USSR has lent its considerable authority to moves to have South Africa and Rhodesia banned from all international tournaments; and it is largely through Soviet action that international federations (for instance, those for equestrian sport, swimming and sports medicine) have introduced articles into their statutes proscribing racial, political, religious or any other form of discrimination. It is not unusual for Soviet competitors to forfeit matches rather than play against white South Africans and Rhodesians. There is little doubt that such Soviet action wins much sympathy among certain circles in the Third World, which see in the USSR a champion of their cause. This attitude is reinforced by frequent Soviet references to the multinational nature of Soviet sport: 'The Soviet Olympic delegation of 1972 was a mirror of Soviet multinational sport. Patriotism and collectivism, friendship and mutual assistance have become integral to the outlook of our athletes. They therefore look upon racial discrimination in sport as monstrous and inhuman.'[9] 'The internationalist character of socialist sport,' the conclusion is drawn, 'has a great impact on the newly liberated ex-colonies.'[10]

## Conclusion

The pattern of foreign sports competition involving the

USSR has closely followed the course of Soviet foreign policy. With its control of the sports system, the Soviet leadership has been able to mobilize resources to achieve maximum efficiency in its sports challenge and, hence, to perform what it believes to be paramount political functions. While sport in the West is by no means free of politics or foreign-policy aims, in a centrally planned society like that of the USSR sport clearly occupies a focal position and its functions and interrelationship with the political system are more manifest than in Western societies.

The Soviet Union has demonstrated that the highest realization of human potential can be most effectively achieved through the planned application of society's resources. It has attained this goal in sport (and in many other fields of human endeavour and excellence – musicianship, for example), and its achievements have been inspired by the deliberate and quite plausible intention of demonstrating the superiority of its system. In general, in the Western world the whipping up of popular fervour in sport has, by accident or by design, often resulted in the sacrifice of the sporting (and Olympic) ideal on the altar of national or ethnic chauvinism. In the USSR, thanks partly to its multinational population, this has been largely avoided; it is not some innate ethnic or national superiority that has been seen to triumph, but a political system.

That Soviet international sporting contacts are in general subordinate to the general lines of Soviet foreign policy is indisputable, and this has led on occasion to political opportunism. But it is equally true that sport and the Olympic movement have assumed, as a result, a pre-eminent role in moral leadership in the context of world politics as exemplified by the apartheid issue. The increasing political isolation of South Africa in world affairs must be due in no small measure to the catalytic role played by the now very extensive boycott of sporting contacts with

*Moscow central swimming pool, open all year round, even at subzero
temperatures*

that country, to which the Soviet Union has made a
notable, even leading, contribution.

## NOTES

[1] The Third or Communist International was set up in Moscow in
March 1919, with the avowed objective of working to spread
communism throughout the world. As Trotsky put it: 'If today
the centre of the Third International lies in Moscow, then
tomorrow . . . it will shift westward: to Berlin, to Paris, to
London' (*The Age of Permanent Revolution*, New York, 1964,
p. 131).

[2] *Teoriya i praktika fizicheskoi kul'tury*, No. 1, 1973, p. 8.

[3] *Integratsiya v sporte* (Moscow, 1978), p. 98.

[4] *Ibid.*, p. 99.

[5] *Mezhdunarodnoye sportivnoye dvizhenie* (Moscow, 1973), p. 177.

[6] *Ibid.*, p. 182.

[7] *Sport v SSSR*, No. 12, 1972, p. 24.

[8] *Fizkul'tura i sport*, No. 3, 1971, p. 1.

[9] *Sportivnaya zhizn' Rossii*, No. 11, 1972, p. 7. The further point was made that representatives of twenty-six Soviet nationalities, including those from all fifteen republics, were present at the 1972 Munich Olympics.

[10] *Sport v SSSR*, No. 2, 1973, p. 19.

# Appendix 1

## GTO — Stage 3:
## 'Sila i muzhestvo' ('Strength and Courage')
## (for Boys and Girls 16—18)

*Academic requirements* (to be examined)

1. To have a knowledge of the subject 'Physical Culture and Sport in the USSR'.
2. To know and carry out the rules for personal and public hygiene.
3. To master the programme for initial military training (including the section on the protection from weapons of mass destruction) and to wear a gas mask for 1 hour, or undergo specialist training in a DOSAAF organisation, or obtain an applied technical speciality (for boys). Girls should know the basic rules of civil defence and wear a gas mask for one hour.
4. To be able to explain the importance of and perform a set of morning exercises.

*Physical exercises: qualifying standards*

| | Boys | | Girls | |
|---|---|---|---|---|
| Type of exercise | Silver Badge | Gold Badge | Silver Badge | Gold Badge |
| 1. Run 100 m (sec) | 14.2 | 13.5 | 16.2 | 15.4 |
| 2. Run 500 m (min/sec) | – | – | 2.00 | 1.50 |
|     1000 m (min/sec) | 3.30 | 3.20 | – | – |
|     or | | | | |
|     Skate 500 m (min/sec) | 1.25 | 1.15 | 1.30 | 1.20 |

| Type of exercise | Boys | | Girls | |
|---|---|---|---|---|
| | Silver Badge | Gold Badge | Silver Badge | Gold Badge |
| 3. Long jump (cm) | 440 | 480 | 340 | 375 |
| or | | | | |
| High jump (cm) | 125 | 135 | 105 | 115 |
| 4. Hurl a hand-grenade of | | | | |
| 500 gm (m) | – | – | 21 | 25 |
| 700 gm (m) | 35 | 40 | – | – |
| or putt the shot of | | | | |
| 4 kg (m/cm) | – | – | 6.00 | 6.80 |
| 5 kg (m) | 8 | 10 | – | – |
| 5. Ski 3 km (min) | – | – | 20 | 18 |
| 5 km (min) | 27 | 25 | – | – |
| or 10 km (min) | 57 | 52 | – | – |
| In snow-free regions: | | | | |
| Run cross country 3 km (min) | – | – | 20 | 18 |
| 6 km (min) | 35 | 32 | – | – |
| or cycle cross country | | | | |
| 10 km (min) | – | – | 30 | 27 |
| 20 km (min) | 50 | 46 | – | – |
| 6. Swim 100 m (min/sec) | 2.00 | 1.45 | 2.15 | 2.00 |
| 7. Press-ups | 8 | 12 | – | – |
| Pull-ups | – | – | 10 | 12 |
| 8. Fire a small-bore rifle at 25 m (points) | 33 | 40 | 30 | 37 |
| or at 50 m (points) | 30 | 37 | 27 | 34 |
| or fire a heavy weapon | Satis-factory | Well | Satis-factory | Well |
| 9. Tourist hike with test of tourist knowledge and orienteering | 1 hike of 20 km or 2 hikes of 12 km | 1 hike of 25 km or 2 hikes of 15 km | 1 hike of 20 km or 2 hikes of 12 km | 1 hike of 25 km or 2 hikes of 15 km |
| 10. Obtain a sports ranking in: | | | | |
| (a) motor car, motor boat, motorcycle, gliding, parachuting, aeroplane, helicopter, sub-aqua or | – | III | – | III |

| Type of exercise | Boys | | Girls | |
| --- | --- | --- | --- | --- |
| | Silver Badge | Gold Badge | Silver Badge | Gold Badge |
| water sports, biathlon, pentathlon, pistol shooting, radio sport, orienteering, wrestling or boxing; | | | | |
| (b) any other sport | – | II | – | II |

*Note:* For the Gold Badge, one must complete not less than 7 qualifying standards at Gold Badge level and 2 standards at Silver Badge level (except item 10). Girls who have completed a first-aid training course may forego item 10 for their Gold Badge.

# Appendix 2

## *Syllabus for Undergraduate Teacher–Coaches at the Central Institute of Physical Culture: 1975*

| Discipline | Total number of: exams | tests | Distribution of disciplines by year of course I | II | III | IV |
|---|---|---|---|---|---|---|
| History of the Communist Party of the Soviet Union | 2 | – | + | | | |
| Marxist-Leninist philosophy | 4 | – | | + | | |
| Scientific atheism | 7 | – | | | | + |
| Political economy | 6 | – | | | + | |
| Scientific Communism | – | 8 | | | | + |
| Foreign language | 7 | 4 | + | + | | + |
| Introduction to specialism | – | – | + | | | |
| Biochemistry and sports Biochemistry | 3 | 2 | + | + | | |
| Human anatomy | 2 | – | + | | | |
| Sports morphology | – | 3 | | + | | |
| Biomechanics with fundamentals of sports techniques | – | 4 | | + | | |
| Physiology and sports physiology | 5 | 3 | | + | + | |
| Hygiene and sports hygiene | 6 | 6 | | | + | |
| Sports medicine (medical control, sports pathology) | 8 | 6 | | | + | + |
| Sports massage | – | 4 | | + | | |
| Psychology and sports psychology | 4 | 4 | | + | | |
| Education and history of education | 2 | – | + | | | |
| Theory and method of physical education | 5 | 4 | | + | + | |

| Discipline | Total number of: | | Distribution of disciplines by year of course | | | |
|---|---|---|---|---|---|---|
| | exams | tests | I | II | III | IV |
| Sports coaching | 6 | – | | | + | |
| Biometrics | – | 8 | | | | + |
| Statistics | – | 2 | + | | | |
| History of sport | 1 | – | + | | | |
| Organization, economics and management of sport | 7 | 7 | | | | + |
| Sports amenities | – | 1 | + | | | |
| Film and photography | – | 2 | + | | | |
| Chosen sport and method of teaching it | 8 | 7 | + | + | + | + |
| Additional sports: | | | | | | |
|   Athletics | 2 | 2 | + | | | |
|   Gymnastics | 3 | 3 | + | + | | |
|   Swimming | 3 | 3 | + | | | |
|   Team Sports | 6 | 5 | | + | + | |
|   Skiing | 1 | 1 | + | | | |
|   Weightlifting | – | 1 | + | | | |
| Optional courses* | 7 | 8 | | + | + | |
| Civil defence | – | 8 | | | | + |
| Remedial physical education (for women) | 8 | 7 | | + | + | + |

* These include political education in sport, organization of sports work organization of the international Olympic movement, forecasting sports talent, rehabilitation of work capacity, etc.

In addition to their lectures and seminars, students are required to go on organized visits to museums, exhibitions, and places of revolutionary, war and labour glory. They must prepare dissertations, take part in readings from Lenin, make reports and become acquainted with the working conditions and everyday lives of factory workers. They must also themselves work on state farms and construction sites.

By way of financial support, students receive a state grant of 40 rubles a month in their first three years, and 45 rubles a month in their final year. Students who obtain 'excellent' marks in their tests and take an active part in the social life of the Institute may receive a 15 per cent increment to the ordinary grant – i.e. 50 rubles in the first three years and 56 rubles in the final year. The best students in Year III may be sent abroad to other socialist states for their practical work.

The final examination for students who have completed all academic and other requirements is in two subjects: scientific Communism and physiology. In addition, students must defend their dissertation. Successful students are then awarded the diploma of 'Teacher of Physical Education and Coach in (a particular sport)'.

*Source: Notes for the guidance of Students at the state Central Order of Lenin Institute of Physical Culture* (in Russian) (Moscow, 1975), p. 43.

# Index

172     *Index*